The Effects of Monetary Policy on Mortgage Rates

Office of Policy Analysis and Research
Federal Housing Finance Agency
400 7th Street SW
Washington, D.C. 20024, USA

June 2014

The Effects of Monetary Policy on Mortgage Rates

Abstract

Economic events over the past decade have changed central bank policies in the United States and around the world. The housing and financial markets experienced significant changes as the markets first surpassed historical highs and then underwent a recession grave enough to draw comparison with the Great Depression. To spur recovery, the Federal Reserve first lowered short-term interest rates to near-zero and eventually embarked on several phases of large-scale asset purchases (LSAPs) to lower long-term interest rates and mortgage rates. This paper describes the evolution of the LSAP program and analyzes how interest rates and mortgage rates changed during that time. Both the long-term interest rates and mortgage rates reached historical lows in the post crisis period, primarily due to the Federal Reserve Board's accommodative policies. Two econometric approaches—an event study and a time series model—estimate the market response during each phase of the LSAP program and provide projections of mortgage rates under different shock assumptions. Results suggest that early tapering announcements helped reset interest rates and mortgage rates upwards and any rise in long-term interest rates resulting from unanticipated events (whether related to tapering or not) could lead to further increases in mortgage rates.

Keywords: asset purchase · QE · Federal Reserve · interest rates · mortgage rates · financial projections

JEL Classification: E52 · E44 · G17

Working Paper 14-2 — "The Effects of Monetary Policy on Mortgage Rates"
Executive Summary (E.S.)

E.S.I Purpose

The purpose of this working paper is to study how the Federal Reserve Board's (the Fed's) accommodative monetary policy of large-scale asset purchases (LSAP) and its tapering have affected mortgage rates.

E.S.II Outline

This working paper is split into two main parts.

- The first part describes different LSAP phases and discusses how long-term interest rates and mortgage rates changed during various LSAP phases.

- The second part provides a combined empirical approach of an event study and a dynamic time series model. The event study shows how LSAP announcements, including tapering announcements, have affected the 10-year U.S. Treasury Note rate. The time series model shows how the 30-year fixed rate mortgage (FRM) rate changed during different LSAP phases with the 10-year U.S. Treasury Note rate. It also provides projections of how the 30-year FRM rate might change from a range of shocks to the 10-year U.S. Treasury Note due to unexpected events.

E.S.III Key Points

- During the LSAP program, long-term interest rates and mortgage rates were lower than they would have been without the Fed policies. In fact, they were at a historical low.

- However, other macroeconomic and financial factors, in addition to the Fed policies, also affected long-term interest rates and mortgages rates.

- The first round of the LSAP program had a significant effect in lowering long-term interest rates and mortgage rates as the program intended. In comparison, subsequent rounds of the LSAP program did not lower long-term rates and mortgage rates to the same extent. This may have been because the subsequent rounds were anticipated.

- As expected, the Fed announcements suggesting tapering in mid-2013 helped reset long-term interest rates and mortgage rates upwards. The tapering announcements at the end of 2013 had little effect on long-term interest rates and mortgage rates because the market had already begun adjusting to tapering with earlier announcements.

- Future tapering announcements are unlikely to significantly affect long-term interest rates and mortgage rates unless such announcements convey unanticipated news or changes.

- An unanticipated tapering announcement can increase long-term interest rates and mortgage rates further. For example, a 10 basis point shock to the 10-year U.S. Treasury Note yield could increase the 30-year FRM rate by approximately 75 basis points a quarter later.

I Introduction

Monetary policy instruments employed by central bankers have changed since the 2007–2008 financial crisis. As the crisis began in 2007, the Federal Reserve Board (or the "Fed") began gradually reducing the federal funds rate. When the federal funds rate approached the lower bound of zero towards the end of 2008, the Fed adopted a new monetary policy strategy: large-scale asset purchases (LSAP). The reasoning was that open market purchases of agency and Treasury securities by the Fed would increase the prices and decrease the yields of those securities and thus make private securities, in comparison, more attractive to investors. As a result, financial markets would again achieve better liquidity and reduced credit constraints and ultimately consumer confidence and the economy would improve. Improving the housing market was also a specific goal of the LSAP program.[1] With the LSAP program as the policy lever, the Fed intended to artificially lower mortgage rates and stimulate housing recovery in the midst of a crisis. Indeed, mortgage rates during the LSAP program were lower than they likely would have been without the Fed policies, which undoubtedly contributed to the housing recovery of the past few years.

The Fed's purchases first focused on debt from government-sponsored agencies and then, in a more sustained manner, on a combination of mortgage backed securities (MBS) from the agencies and long-term U.S. Treasury securities.[2] In the span of five years, the LSAP program has undergone several phases commonly referred to as various stages of "quantitative easing" (or "QE") and a "Twist." There was increased speculation that the Fed would curb the LSAP program in the latter half of 2013 after the Fed first suggested it in May and June.[3]

---

[1] For motivation, goals and an overview of the LSAP program summarized in this introduction, see former Chairman Bernanke's speech to the Federal Reserve Bank of Kansas City Economic Symposium in Jackson Hole, Wyoming on August 31, 2012. It specifically lists improving the housing market as a goal.

[2] The government-sponsored agencies included the Federal National Mortgage Association (or "Fannie Mae") and the Federal Home Loan Mortgage Corporation (or "Freddie Mac"), and the twelve Federal Home Loan Banks. The Fed purchased MBS from the following agencies: Fannie Mae, Freddie Mac and Ginnie Mae.

[3] For example, see the Financial Times from June 17, 2013.

The Fed finally announced its decision to taper the LSAP program last December. The Fed's tapering of the LSAP program should be expected to raise long-term interest rates and mortgage rates to a higher, sustainable level.[4]

A series of research papers have provided insights about the LSAP program while retrospectively exploring their effects on mortgage rates (Hancock & Passmore 2011, 2012) and interest rate yields (Gagnon et al. 2011; Krishnamurthy & Vissing-Jorgensen 2011; Swanson 2011; D'Amico et al. 2012; Thornton 2013). A number of these papers have employed the event study methodology to draw links between public announcements and interest rate movements. This paper also uses the event study methodology. The estimation strategies in exisiting literature, however, have captured only contemporaneous relationships from a particular point in time.[5] As the Fed's purchases and holdings recede, there will be an increasing need to broaden our understanding of how the LSAP programs affect current and also future markets. An empirical analysis that captures the dynamic relationship between long-term interest rates and mortgage rates could help provide insights about whether information was fully priced into a series or what might happen after an unexpected shock (like a public announcement). Furthermore, a dynamic approach can provide projections about how future rates might evolve without placing too much structure on a system. This paper employs such a dynamic framework—specifically vector autoregression (VAR)—in addition to the event study methodolgy and enhances the existing literature.

The paper begins with some background about the LSAP program, long-term interest rates, and mortgage rates. Section II describes the four main phases of the Fed's LSAP program. Details are provided about each phase as well as the current status of tapering and asset

---

[4]It should be noted that the majority of the FOMC participants anticipate higher fed funds rate by the end of 2015 based on the FOMC announcements from March 19, 2014. See the Fed's projections and assessments.

[5]An exception is a study by Gagnon et al. (2011) that discusses details of the LSAP program and uses DOLS to model the dynamic relationships between variables like interest rates, unemployment, and inflation.

---

holdings. Section III discusses how interest rates and mortgage rates changed during the LSAP program and how other macroeconomic and financial factors may have affected them in addition to the Fed's monetary policy.

The main focus of this paper is to estimate effects of the Fed's monetary policy approach first on long-term interest rates and then on mortgage rates. A two-part empirical approach attempts this task in Section IV with some retrospective discussion and a glance forward. Subsection IV.A uses an event study to show how important announcements and events have affected the 10-year U.S. Treasury yield by isolating the effects of the LSAP program. The first round of LSAP program, in contrast to subsequent rounds, had a significant effect in lowering the 10-year U.S. Treasury yield as the program was designed to do. The tapering announcements of December 2013 and January 2014 only had minimal effect on the 10-year Treasury yield because, by that time, the market had already adjusted in response to earlier unanticipated announcements about tapering in May and June 2013. Future tapering announcements are also likely to have minimal effect on the 10-year Treasury unless they convey substantial changes to the program. Subsection IV.B employs dynamic time series estimations to provide in-sample projections for long-term interest rates and mortgage rates during the past LSAP phases to show how mortgage rates change with long-term interest rates. Mortgage rates moved in tandem with the 10-year Treasury yield during different phases of the LSAP program. The time series model also provides out-of-sample projections in future periods under different shock scenarios. Any unanticipated tapering announcement could certainly increase mortgage rates further. These implications and other empirical considerations are discussed in Subsection IV.C. Lastly, Section V concludes the paper with final remarks.

II How did the LSAP program evolve?

When the financial crisis began in 2007, the Federal Reserve first sought to spur economic recovery with traditional policy levers: it initially reduced the discount rate and extended loan terms to banks and it also began gradually reducing the target federal funds rate. When the target federal funds rate dropped close to zero by late 2008 and effectively ended the use of traditional monetary policy levers, the Fed then embarked on a new program to support stronger mortgage market and economic recovery by putting further downward pressure on long-term interest rates and, particularly, mortgage interest rates. In essence, the Fed's program artificially lowered rates relative to what they would have been in its absence in order to stimulate mortgage market recovery. As a result, the recent tapering program is likely to return the rates more closely to what they would have been. The increase in mortgage rates will likely have an effect on the housing market over time. The Fed's LSAP program entailed purchasing long-term securities issued by the U.S. government and long-term debt and securities issued by the government-sponsored enterprises. This Fed program of large-scale asset purchases has become known popularly as QE and has been rolled out in four separate phases.

II.A The LSAP phases

The LSAP program was designed to lower long-term interest rates and help stimulate economic recovery through the "portfolio balance channel" and the "signaling effect".[6] Through the portfolio balance channel, the Fed's LSAP program was expected to reduce the public supply of long-duration assets such as U.S. Treasury securities and agency mortgage-backed securities (MBS) thus reducing long-term interest rates. The intention was to encourage investors to shift to other types of assets such as stocks and corporate bonds and, subsequently,

---

[6]The MBS purchases were intended to specifically and directly affect mortgage yields. The evolution of the U.S. monetary policy since late 2007 and the rationale for it is summarized in former Chairman Bernanke's speech at the Federal Reserve Bank of Kansas City Economic Symposium in Jackson Hole, Wyoming on August 31, 2012.

---

stimulate economic activity.[7] Through the signaling effect, the content and timing of the Fed communications to begin or expand the LSAP program were also designed to convince investors and other market participants about the Fed's commitment to its accommodative policy stance.[8] The Fed developed and refined the LSAP program over more than five years and across four distinct phases as described below.[9]

QE1

The first phase of LSAP, later called "QE1", was announced on November 25, 2008 and the Fed purchases started on December 1, 2008. The purchases originally consisted of agency debt and MBS and were scheduled to end by December 2009. The Fed purchase of agency debt and MBS was designed to support the housing markets by decreasing the cost and increasing the availability of credit for buying houses, which in turn was expected to improve general financial market conditions.[10] This program was further expanded on March 18, 2009 to purchase greater amounts of agency debt and MBS as well as to purchase long-term Treasury securities for six months. The addition of long-term Treasury securities purchases was meant to improve conditions in the private credit markets as well as to ward off defla-

---

[7]The portfolio balance channel has also been described as some combination of "scarcity", "preferred-habitat", "liquidity" and "safety" channels or effects (D'Amico et al. 2012; Krishnamurthy & Vissing-Jorgensen 2011).

[8]This channel is also been called the "expectation" channel or effect. In addition, academic articles have identified the "duration" channel as well as other channels of how the LSAP affect the financial markets (D'Amico et al. 2012; Krishnamurthy & Vissing-Jorgensen 2011). This paper does not describe these channels or develop any theoretical models or foundations on how the LSAP program can influence the housing and financial markets. Rather, this paper aims to provide estimates of how the LSAP program and its tapering affects interest rates within the larger context of how other external events such as the European sovereign debt crises and the U.S. fiscal policy woes also affect interest rates, at times negating and dwarfing the effects of the LSAP program.

[9]There is no designated or single source for complete details about the LSAP program. Still, much data and information can be gathered from a handful of resources. For example, specific monetary actions are documented in the annual reports on domestic open market operations by the Federal Reserve Bank of New York. A timeline of events in the earlier LSAP phases was put together by the Federal Reserve Bank of St. Louis (2009). In addition, early phases of the Fed's LSAP program in the context of the 2007–2008 financial crisis have been discussed by several sources (Gagnon et al. 2011; Hancock & Passmore 2011; D'Amico et al. 2012). The LSAP details in this section and paper were obtained from Federal Reserve Bank of New York and verified using the transaction data downloaded from the Federal Reserve Bank of New York website and the Federal Reserve website.

[10]This was done in conjunction with smaller purchases by the Treasury. In both cases, part of the intent was to emphasize government support for the GSEs.

---

tion. The program was extended on September 23, 2009 to continue agency debt and MBS purchase until March 31, 2010.

Overall, the Fed purchased three types of agency and government assets on the open market during QE1: 1) agency debt from Fannie Mae (FNMA), Freddie Mac (FHLMC) and the Federal Home Loan Banks (FHLB); 2) MBS from Fannie Mae, Freddie Mac and Ginnie Mae (GNMA); and 3) long-term U.S. Treasury securities. They are depicted in Figure 1 as red, blue, and green lines respectively. Figure 1 presents the monthly dollar volume of asset purchases by the Fed in the top half of the panel using solid lines and sales in the bottom half using dashed lines. The chart is separated into four sections by QE period with a gray vertical area denoting the QE1 phase.

Figure 1: The Federal Reserve's large-scale asset purchase and sale volumes

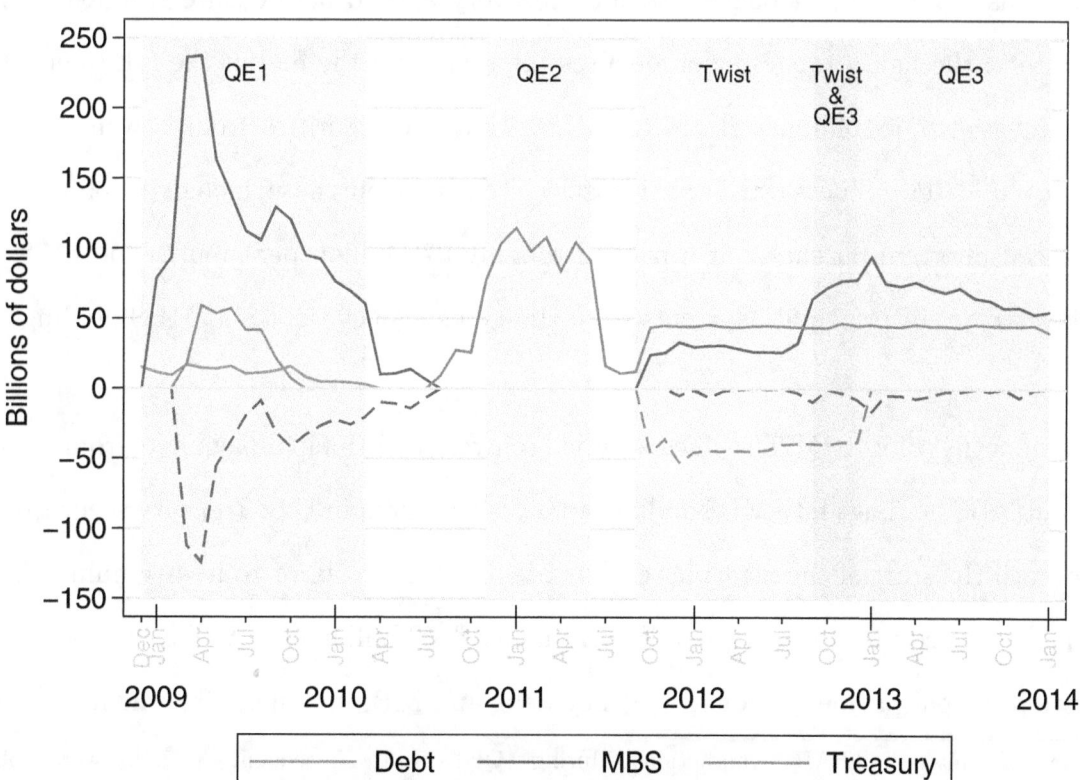

Source: The Federal Reserve Bank of New York.
Note: Purchases are solid lines and sales are dashed lines.

The three different types of Fed purchases have varied in size.[11] The Fed purchased a total of $172 billion in agency debt from December 2008 to March 2010, $1.85 trillion of agency MBS from January 2009 to July 2010 and $300 billion of long-term U.S. Treasury securities from March 2009 to October 2009. The MBS purchases comprised $1.25 trillion of announced net purchases, which ended in March 2010, and about $600 billion in reinvestment of principal payments from the Fed's agency debt and MBS holdings, which continued until July 2010. From January 2009 to July 2010, the Fed also sold $600 billion of its MBS holdings as part of the dollar roll transactions.[12] But this was not a sale of Fed's holdings.

QE2

The second phase of LSAP, called "QE2", was announced on November 3, 2010 and ended on June 30, 2011. During QE2, the Fed purchased only U.S. Treasury securities. The goal of QE2 was to promote stronger economic recovery and to help ensure stability of prices. In Figure 1, the light orange region denotes the start and the end of the QE2 period. The Fed purchased $778 billion of long-term U.S. Treasury securities from November 3, 2010 to June 30, 2011. The total U.S. Treasury securities purchase included $600 billion in announced program purchase, at a pace of roughly $75 billion per month, and $178 billion as reinvestment of principal payments from the Fed's agency debt and MBS holdings.

Several months prior to QE2, the Fed stopped reinvesting principal payments from its agency debt and MBS holdings into MBS and began investing them in U.S. Treasury securities. This lasted until the start of the next phase. Outside of QE2 (i.e. prior to its beginning and after it ended), the Fed purchased a sizeable but smaller $103 billion of U.S. Treasury securities to reinvest principal payments from its agency debt and MBS holdings. The figure also shows

---

[11]The amount of LSAP transactions during QE1 and subsequent phases were obtained by aggregating transaction level data from the Federal Reserve Bank of New York at http://www.ny.frb.org/markets/openmarket.html.

[12]A dollar roll transaction is purchase or sale of an agency MBS for delivery in the current month, with the simultaneous agreement to sell or purchase substantially similar (although not necessarily the same) securities on a specified future date. It is not a sale of the Fed's holdings.

---

that this period did not include sale of any of the three types of assets held by the Fed.

Twist

The third phase popularly called "Operation Twist" or the "Twist" was announced on September 21, 2011 and ended on December 31, 2012. During the "Twist", the Fed purchased $668 billion of U.S. Treasury securities with maturities of six to 30 years and sold close to $634 billion of U.S. Treasury securities with maturities of three months to three years.[13] The Twist, like QE2, was also designed to support stronger economic recovery and ensure stable inflation environment. This program, called more formally the Maturity Extension Program, overlapped with nearly four months of QE3 (see next section). The Twist-only period is denoted by a light blue area in Figure 1 and the overlap of the Twist and QE3 periods is denoted by a light purple area. During the entire Twist phase, principal payments from the Fed's agency debt and MBS holdings were reinvested into MBS securities once again. During the Twist and prior to the start of QE3, the Fed purchased roughly $312 million of MBS as reinvestment. In addition to the sale of short-term Treasury securities, the Fed also sold $ 23 billion of MBS during the Twist-only period as part of the dollar roll transactions. Similar to QE1, this was not a sale of Fed's holdings.

QE3

The fourth and the current phase, popularly called "QE3" was announced on September 13, 2012. QE3 is depicted by the light purple and light green areas in Figure 1. In September 2012, the Fed started purchasing MBS securities at the rate of $40 billion per month under QE3 with the intention of supporting stronger recovery and stability of inflation. The Fed also continued to purchase additional MBS as reinvestment of principal payments. On December 12, 2012, the Fed announced further purchase of long-term U.S. Treasury securities, with the same goal of supporting stronger economic recovery and stable inflation. The Fed

---

[13]In addition, about $33 million of U.S. long-term securities purchased by the Fed during the Twist was redeemed by the end of 2012.

---

began purchasing U.S. Treasury securities at the rate of \$45 billion per month under QE3 in January 2013, after the Twist ended.[14] The purchases continued at this rate until the Fed decided to taper its asset purchase program at the end of 2013. On December 18, 2013, the Fed announced it would reduce the monthly purchases to \$35 billion of agency MBS and \$40 billion of Treasury securities in January 2014. Similarly, the Fed announced on January 29, 2014 that it would reduce the monthly purchases to \$30 billion of agency MBS and \$35 billion of Treasury securities in February 2014.

From September 2012 to January 2014, the Fed purchased \$1.2 trillion of agency MBS and \$580 billion of long-term U.S. Treasury securities under QE3. The Fed also sold \$63 billion of its MBS holdings as part of the dollar roll transactions.

As discussed above, the Fed's LSAP (or QE) program consisted of agency debt, agency MBS and U.S. Treasury securities purchases. Each of the three types of asset purchases is described in greater detail in Appendix A, including distributions depicted in Figure 8. The next section describes the Fed's asset holdings and further discusses its QE3 tapering activity.

II.B   Tapering and the Fed's asset holdings

The "tapering" of the Fed's LSAP program can be viewed as having two main components: 1) reduction in the pace of purchases resulting in an end to the program at a future date (essentially the "flow"), and 2) liquidation of the Fed's holdings from over five years of asset purchases (essentially the "stock"). The Fed started slowing the rate of asset purchase in 2014. However, the Fed's asset holdings are quite large and it could take a long time to decrease their size. The recent tapering program is expected to offset the reduction

---

[14]A few resources have used the term "QE4" to refer to the period after January 2013 when the U.S. Treasury securities purchases went to a rate of \$45 billion per month. This paper identifies it as a part of QE3.

in mortgage rates from the LSAP program and the increase in mortgage rates may limit housing market activities over time. This section will discuss the current status of tapering and describe the current size of the Fed's asset holdings.

As mentioned above, the Fed decreased its monthly rate of purchase for agency MBS from $40 billion to $35 billion in January 2014 and then to $30 billion in February 2014. Similarly, the Fed decreased its monthly rate of purchase for U.S. Treasury securities from $45 billion to $40 billion in January 2014 and $35 billion in February 2014. The Fed is expected to continue tapering its purchases gradually over time as economic conditions improve but it has not set a strict schedule of decreases in monthly purchases. The Fed has explained its slowing of the rate of asset purchases as a reflection of the current status of improved outlook on economic conditions, particularly for the labor market. But it has been keen to point out that the purchases and tapering are not on a "preset course" and the Fed has not made statements about future asset sales. Future tapering will depend on the Fed's assessment on the outlook for the labor market and inflation as well as the suitability of the program going forward. The Fed has indicated that it will take a "balanced approach consistent with its longer-run goals of maximum employment and inflation of 2 percent."[15]

Figure 2 tracks the Fed's holdings of different asset classes since the start of LSAP program on a weekly basis. As of January 31, 2014, the Fed held $54.9 billion in agency debt, $1.5 trillion in agency MBS and $2.2 trillion in U.S. Treasury securities.[16] The Fed's asset holdings have continued to increase over time for three reasons. First, asset purchases have slowed but they have not stopped. Second, even though the Fed has sold some of its assets, primarily during QE1 and the Twist, asset sales other than those during the Twist have been relatively small and a part of dollar roll transactions rather than outright sale of the

---

[15]The current tapering program and Fed intentions were outlined by Chair Yellen in the Semiannual Monetary Policy Report to Congress on February 11, 2014.

[16]The data on Fed's holdings was downloaded from the Federal Reserve Bank of New York website.

Fed's holdings. Third, the Fed has continued to reinvest principal payments from its agency debt and MBS holdings into additional MBS purchases.[17] It is reasonable to expect that the Fed may liquidate its massive asset holdings in addition to the current program of tapering the rate of asset purchases. Liquidation of the Fed's assets holding is an ultimately critical component of decreasing the Fed's footprint in the market. But it is not clear when or how the Fed will start to liquidate its asset holdings or simply let them run off. Therefore, while liquidation of the Fed's assets holding is a critical component of tapering, this paper is limited to discussing the possible effects of only the reduction in the rate of asset purchases, and not any asset liquidation program.

Figure 2: The Federal Reserve's cumulative asset holdings from LSAP

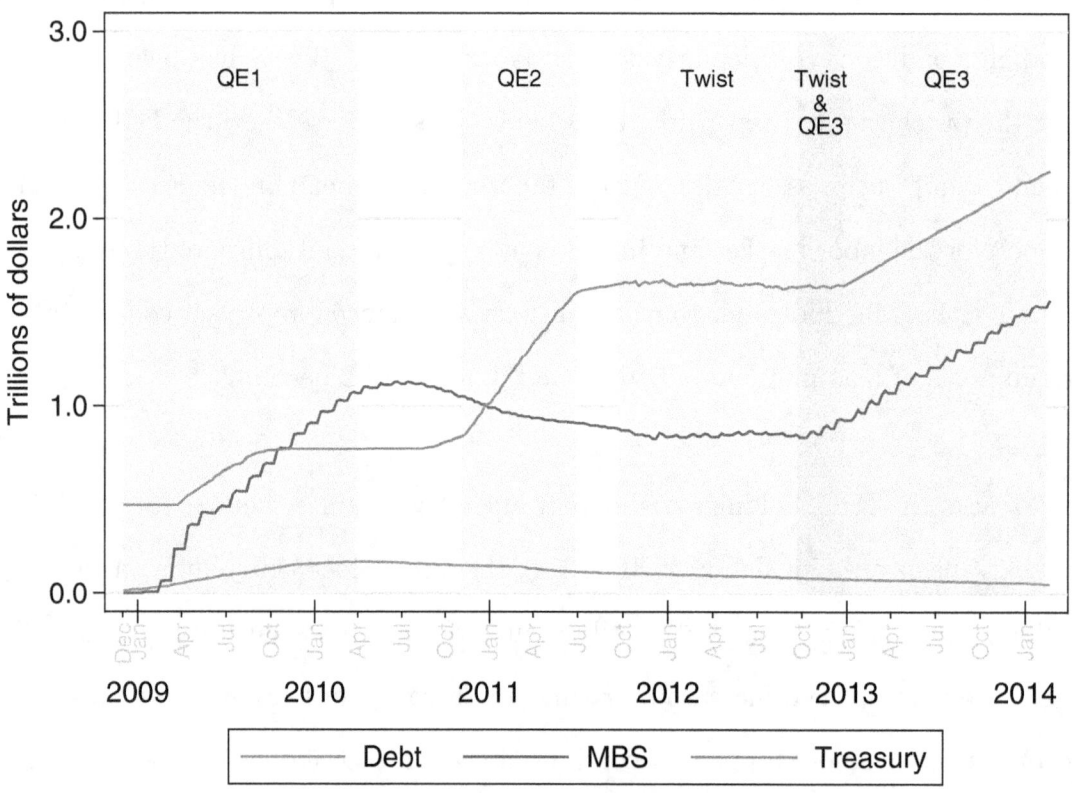

Source: The Federal Reserve Bank of New York.

[17]As discussed in the previous section, the Fed reinvested the principal payments in U.S. Treasury securities during QE2.

III How did interest rates and mortgage rates change during the LSAP program?

Housing and financial markets— mortgage rates in particular—are influenced by long-term interest rates. In fact, as stated in the prior section, the first-order goal of the Fed's LSAP program was to lower long-term interest rates, partially in order to stimulate the economic and housing recovery. Hence, tapering of the LSAP program, all else equal, should be expected to entail some reversal of interest rate and mortgage rate decreases from the program. Furthermore, the LSAP program can be expected to have had varying effects over time given the multiple phases and components of the program. However, the LSAP program is not the only factor which affects long-term interest rates and mortgage rates. Forces other than the LSAP program may affect rates in an opposing direction that reduces or even cancels out the effects of quantitative easing. For example, long-term rates are also affected by other macroeconomic factors such as employment, debt, the international economy, geopolitical tensions, and financial or stock market performance. Econometric estimation of the effects of the LSAP program and its tapering is presented in the empirical section. This section, in contrast to the next section, paints the backdrop and discusses long-term interest rates and mortgage rates in the context of the LSAP program, as well as the broader macroeconomic and financial changes.

This section (and the remainder of this paper) focuses primarily on the 10-year U.S. Treasury yield, the 30-year fixed-rate mortgage (FRM) interest rate, and the mortgage-backed securities (MBS) current coupon yield for three main reasons. First, the 10-year U.S. Treasury Note and the current-coupon MBS yields represent the market returns on the assets the Fed purchased as part of the LSAP program and the 30-year FRM rate is broadly indicative of the mortgage prices that the LSAP program was designed to affect via long-term interest rates. Second, the paper rests on the reasoning that the 10-year U.S. Treasury yield reflects changes in monetary policy, and it has a direct influence on 30-year FRM rates, which in turn affect MBS current-coupon yields.[18] Third, these particular series are reported on a daily basis, which is useful for econometric analysis performed in the later sections.

10-year U.S. Treasury Note

The 10-year U.S. Treasury Note is the most popular debt instrument in the world and it is highly traded in the secondary market. It is often used as the benchmark security to measure the return of long-term assets and is considered risk-free. The yield of the 10-year U.S. Treasury Note is effectively the risk-free long-term interest rate. As described in the previous section, the LSAP program was designed to lower the yields of long-term U.S. Treasury securities, including, but not limited to, the 10-year U.S. Treasury Note.

Figure 3 presents the time series of the 10-year Treasury yield (green line) along with the S&P 500 stock index (blue line). After the Fed cut the target federal funds rate to 1 percent, the 10-year Treasury yield started declining from about 4 percent on October 31, 2008. In November, this decline coincided with some media speculation about the Fed launching the new LSAP program.[19] The Fed, in fact, had started purchasing agency debt outright as early as September 19, 2008.[20] In addition, as the stock market continued to retreat, there was an additional flight to quality move from the stock market into U.S. Treasuries. On November 25, 2008, when the Fed first announced the LSAP program, the 10-year Treasury yield dropped 24 basis points (bps) in one day and continued to drop until several days after agency debt purchases started on December 1, 2008.[21] In fact, the 10-year Treasury yield dropped to a period low at 2.08 percent on December 18, 2008—two days after the Fed

---

[18]In fact, the 30-year FRM rate, the 10-year Treasury yield, and the current-coupon MBS yield are highly correlated as discussed more later in this section. In particular, the spread between the 30-year FRM rate and the 10-year Treasury yield at a given time is priced by the market to capture the perceived riskiness at that time of the 30-year FRM relative the 10-year Treasury yield, the risk-free benchmark.

[19]For example, see the Reuters article from November 14, 2008.

[20]The first agency debt purchase transaction in the Fed data is from September 19, 2008.

[21]One basis point (or bps) is one hundredth of one percent.

Figure 3: Historical Treasury and S&P 500

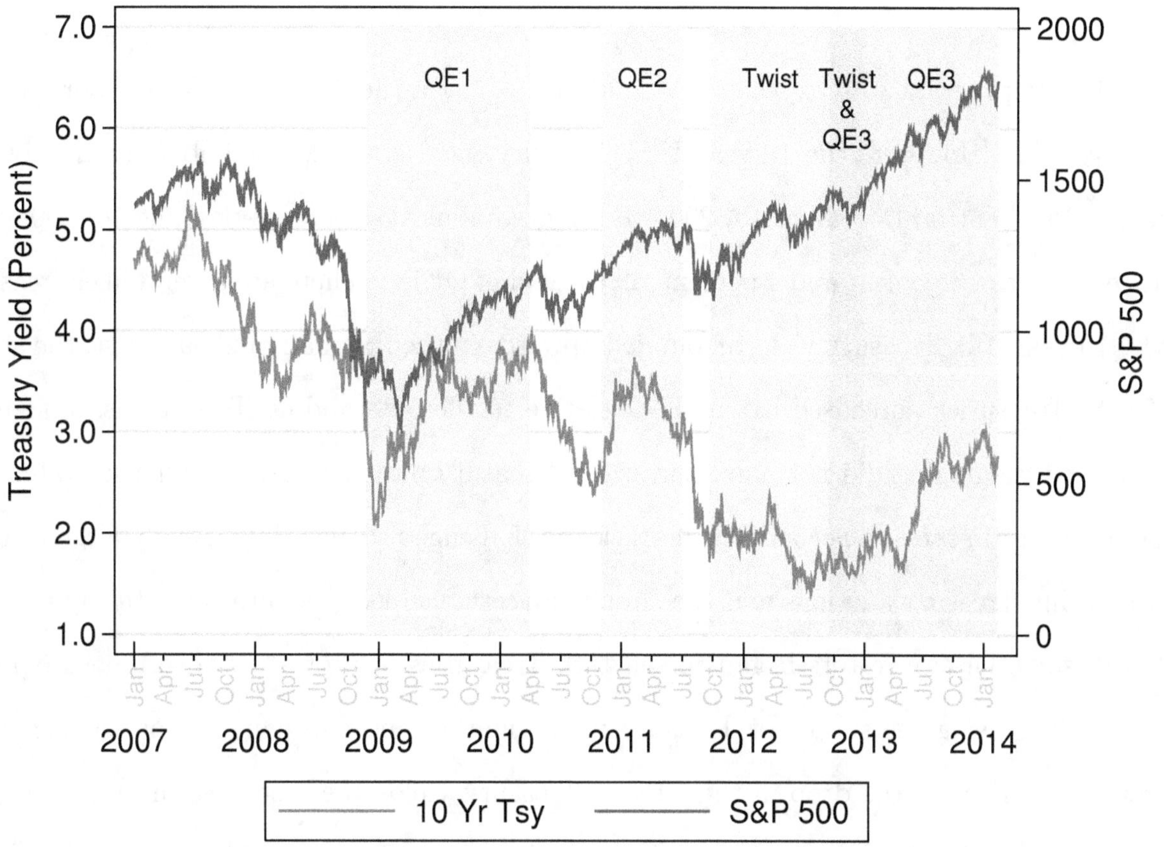

Source: U.S. Treasury and Bloomberg.

reiterated its intention to purchase MBS securities in a Federal Open Market Committee (FOMC) announcement and further reduced the target federal funds rate to between zero and 0.25 percent. On March 18, 2009, when the Fed announced the expansion of the agency debt and MBS purchases and addition of U.S. securities purchase, the 10-year Treasury yield dropped 51 bps in a single day. These decreases in yields (i.e. increases in prices) of U.S. Treasury securities were likely the result of the Fed's strong signaling of its accommodative monetary policy amidst financial and economic turmoil in the marketplace.

The LSAP program was expected to continue to lower the 10-year U.S. Treasury yields during QE1. However, the 10-year U.S. Treasury yield started to climb from the low of nearly 2 percent on December 18, 2008 to a high of almost 4 percent on June 10, 2009 and stayed between 3 percent and 4 percent till the end of QE1.[22] There are several likely reasons why 10-year U.S. Treasury yield rebounded upwards in the first half of 2009. First, the share of U.S. Treasuries purchased by the Fed relative to the outstanding Treasury issuance was small and the market did not judge the size of Treasury purchases to be sufficient to further lower long-term rates.[23] Second, the market was challenged to absorb unusually large volume of monthly Treasury auctions and the supply concerns helped pressure the rates upwards.[24] Third, some large investors began to sell U.S. Treasuries in protest of government policies further increasing the supply of Treasury in the market and subsequently pressuring rates upwards.[25] Fourth, the drop in the 10-year Treasury yields (i.e. increase in prices) during the early months of QE1 encouraged investors to move to stocks and corporate bonds as

---

[22]During QE1, the yield on the 10-year Treasury averaged 3.30 percent with a standard deviation of 45 bps.

[23]In fact, the share of U.S. Treasury securities purchased by the Fed relative to the outstanding Treasury issuances was only about 7 percent. That amount was much smaller than the roughly 18 percent share of the Fed's MBS purchase relative to the outstanding MBSs. The Fed's share of Treasury securities is available on the Securities Industry and Financial Markets Association website. Discussions of QE1 Treasury purchases being small in size and effect were highlighted in articles, such as those published by *The Economist* and the St. Louis Fed.

[24]Concerns about the Treasury supply were highlighted by sources like the *Financial Times* and *The Telegraph*.

[25]These investors were known as "bond vigilantes." The roles of such large investors were outlined by news sources like *The Wall Street Journal*.

---

intended by the Fed.[26] When the stock market started the upswing from a low on March 9, 2009, investors moved more money out of U.S. Treasuries and into the stock market, as shown by the steady increase in both the S&P 500 Index and the 10-year Treasury yields in Figure 3. Finally, as the end of QE1 approached, investors anticipated that future yields would be higher.[27] In aggregate, these macroeconomic and financial factors substantially offset the effects of the LSAP program on the 10-year U.S. Treasury yield.

When QE1 ended, the expectation was that the long-term interest rates would increase. However, the sovereign debt crises started to take hold in Europe, particularly in Greece.[28] As a result, there was a flight to quality into U.S. Treasury securities and the yields of the 10-year U.S. Treasury Note started to drop.[29] The stock market also retreated somewhat at this time and the U.S. Treasuries benefitted.[30] In addition, after former Chairman Bernanke's speech in Jackson Hole, Wyoming on August 27, 2010, there was increased market expectation for a second round of the LSAP program, which contributed towards keeping long-term interest rates low.[31] Again, these macroeconomic and financial factors likely obscured the pure effect of the end of QE1 on long-term interest rates. The yield on the 10-year U.S. Treasury Note dropped from a high around 4 percent (when QE1 ended) to between 2.4 and 2.8 percent (in the period after the Jackson Hole speech and prior to QE2).

When QE2 was launched on November 3, 2010, the 10-year Treasury yield did not react immediately and lost only 14 bps the next day, falling from 2.67 percent to 2.53 percent. In fact, concerns that the QE2 purchases were going to be relatively modest had already started affecting the 10-year Treasury yield as early as late October. The 10-year Treasury yield

---

[26]Figure 3 shows the stock market rally during QE1. There was a similar rally in the corporate bond market, as reported by *Forbes* on February 10, 2010.

[27]Market expectations were highlighted in sources such as CNN Money on February 17, 2010.

[28]BBC (June 13, 2012) provided a timeline of the Eurozone crises.

[29]For example, see the *Financial Times* article from April 27, 2010.

[30]See the *The New York Times* article from May 6, 2010.

[31]See Business Insider and CNN Money (both with articles from August 27, 2010).

continued to move upwards to reach a high of 3.75 by February 8, 2011.[32] The expectation that the LSAP program would lower the 10-year Treasury yield did not hold until the middle of the QE2 period. There are several likely reasons. First, the size of the Treasury securities to be purchased by the Fed under QE2 was smaller than expected and investors did not react to QE2 as they did at the onset of QE1.[33] Second, resembling the QE1 period, the stock market started to pick up by December 2010, although not as vigorously as during QE1, and investors began retreating from U.S. Treasuries and buying more stocks.[34] However, starting in February, 2011, the yield on the 10-year Treasury Note dropped steadily and ended at 2.88 percent by June 24, 2011, at the tail-end of QE2. The most likely cause for this decrease was the worsening of the sovereign debt crises in Europe, particularly in Portugal, during the QE2 period.[35] As investors again became nervous about Europe, there was a flight to quality move into U.S. Treasuries.[36]

Soon after QE2 ended, the sovereign debt crises in Europe intensified, especially in Greece and resulted in investors making an even larger flight to quality move into U.S. Treasuries.[37] This is likely the main cause of precipitous decline in the yield of 10-year Treasury Note during the period between QE2 and the Twist. The 10-year Treasury fell below 2 percent before the Twist was announced.[38] Another factor that affected the 10-year Treasury yield, albeit only briefly, was the downgrading of the U.S. debt to AA+ from AAA on August 5, 2011.[39]

Just after the Twist started, the 10-year Treasury yield completed its downward trend at a

---

[32]Throughout QE2, the yield on the 10-year Treasury had averaged 3.26 with a standard deviation of 26 bps.

[33]See *Financial Times* (November 3, 2010) and *The Economist* (April 25, 2011).

[34]See the *The Washington Post* article from December 31, 2010.

[35]See the *The Telegraph* article from March 27, 2011.

[36]See the CNN Money article from May 23, 2011.

[37]See the *Financial Times* article from July 12, 2011.

[38]During the between-QE periods, the yield on the 10-year Treasury averaged 2.9 percent with a standard deviation of 51 bps.

[39]See CNN Money (August 5, 2011) and Bloomberg (August 6, 2011).

Figure 4: Historical Treasury and mortgage rates

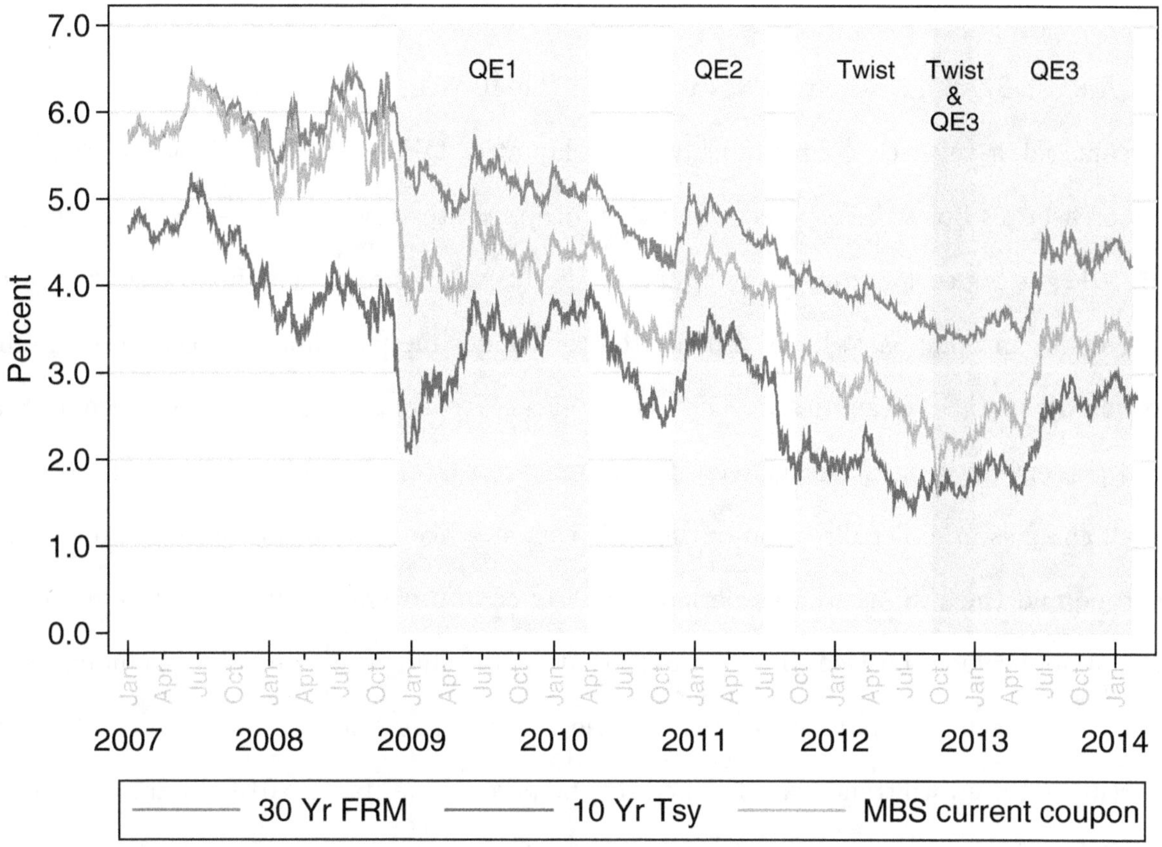

Source: U.S. Treasury and Bloomberg.

low of 1.72 percent on September 22, 2011 and then stayed in the 2 percent range till April 30, 2012. Then it dropped further to an all-time low of 1.43 percent by July 25, 2012 and then rose up again to 1.77 percent before QE3 was announced.[40] The conditions in Europe, including the Greek elections, likely helped to hold down the 10-year Treasury yield because investors continued to favor U.S. Treasuries in their flight to quality during this period.[41] In addition, stagnation of the economy, especially as seen in employment numbers, likely contributed to the drop in the 10-year Treasury yield during this period.[42]

On August 31, 2012, when QE3 was hinted, the 10-year Treasury yield fell 6 bps to 1.57 percent but it reversed course quickly. The day after QE3 started on September 13, 2012, it increased 13 bps to 1.88 percent and then dropped steadily to 1.64 percent on September 26, 2012, as hoped for from a new round of the LSAP program. The fiscal issue in Europe, specifically in Spain, also likely contributed to this decline with another pickup in the flight to quality to U.S. Treasuries.[43] Then the 10-year Treasury yield stayed between 1.58 and 1.84 percent until the Treasury securities purchase program began on January 1, 2013. The small changes in either direction during this time are likely the result of fiscal difficulties in Europe and the U.S. as well as periodic reports of improvements in the U.S. employment. The announcement on December 12, 2012 that QE3 would be expanded to include purchase of Treasury securities had little effect. The yield hovered at 2 percent for a few months before starting a downward trend that dropped to 1.66 percent on May 1, 2013. Fiscal and financial conditions in Europe, particularly in Italy and Cyprus likely precipitated additional flight to quality into U.S. Treasuries at various points during this period.[44] Weak macroeconomic data in April also likely helped continue this decline.[45] Starting May 1, 2013, the 10-year

---

[40]Overall, the 10-year Treasury yield averaged 1.85 percent during the Twist with a standard deviation of 21 bps.

[41]See the Bloomberg article from June 15, 2012.

[42]See the CNN Money article from June 1, 2012.

[43]See Market Watch (October 4, 2012) and Bloomberg (October 3, 2012).

[44]See *Financial Times* (March 31, 2013) and CNBC (March 28, 2013).

[45]See the Reuters article from April 4, 2013.

Treasury yield increased to a high of 2.98 by September 5, 2013 and then dropped closer to 2.85 percent prior to the December 18, 2013 FOMC announcement of tapering. The increase in the 10-year Treasury yield from May to December 2013 was likely caused by two factors. First, periodically favorable employment data came out, which led to more investors in the markets as shown by continued surge of the stock market.[46] Second, there was increasing media speculation surrounding the possibility of an impending tapering of the Fed's asset purchases fueled further by statements from various Fed presidents, as well as the FOMC announcements indicating tapering at a future date as economic conditions improved.[47]

After the December FOMC statement about tapering, the 10-year Treasury yield rose above 3 percent by the end of December 2013. However, in early 2014, the 10-year Treasury yield started dropping once more. This time a major contribution was concern about the developing economies.[48] When the Fed announced further tapering on January 29, 2014, the 10-year Treasury yield dropped 7 bps instead of increasing.[49] In summary, over the course of the LSAP program, the 10-year Treasury changed due to the Fed's monetary policy, as well as other national and international macroeconomic and financial factors.

30-Year Fixed Rate Mortgage

Figure 4 presents the time series of the yield of 10-year Treasury Note (red line) along with the 30-year FRM interest rate (green line) and the yield of current coupon mortgage-backed securities (orange line).[50] The 30-year FRM is the most popular mortgage in the United States for purchasing a single-family house. As a long-term debt instrument, it is influenced heavily by benchmark Treasury yields, particularly the 10-year Treasury yield.

---

[46]See the *USA Today* article from November 8, 2013.

[47]See the *Forbes* article from December 6, 2013.

[48]See the CNBC article from January 31, 2014.

[49]During QE3, until February 2014, the 10-year Treasury yield averaged 2.24 percent with the standard deviation of 47 bps.

[50]The 15-year FRM is not discussed here. Since it is almost perfectly correlated with the 30-year FRM, the two series respond in a very similar way to policy changes.

Not surprisingly, there is a high correlation ($r = 0.95$ from 1990 through 2013) between the daily time series of the 30-year FRM rate and the 10-year Treasury yield. As shown in Figure 4, this relationship remains strong during the sample observation period except during QE1.[51] Since the 10-year Treasury yield is a benchmark risk-free rate for the 30-year FRM rate, the spread between the two is generally a measure of perceived riskiness (e.g. prepayment risk) of the 30-year FRMs. As long as the perceived riskiness of the 30-year FRMs is stable, the correlation between the benchmark 10-year Treasury yield and the 30-year FRM rate is expected to be high. However, during the period when the perceived riskiness of the 30-year FRMs changes, the correlation between the 10-year Treasury yield and the 30-year FRM rate should decline. For example, while the 10-year Treasury had an upward trend during QE1, the 30-year FRM rate declined, indicating a reduction in perceived riskiness of 30-year FRMs during QE1 as shown in Figure 4. The 30-year FRM rate averaged 5.04 percent (with a standard deviation of 18 bps) during QE1, 4.69 percent (with a standard deviation of 21 bps) during QE2, 3.74 percent (with a standard deviation of 25 bps) during the Twist, and 3.95 percent (with a standard deviation of 44 bps) during QE3. Much of the discussion on trends provided for the 10-year Treasury yield is also applicable to the 30-year FRM rate.

Mortgage-Backed Security Yield

The last series (in orange) in Figure 4 is the mortgage-backed securities current coupon yield. Mortgages that make up Fannie Mae, Freddie Mac, and Ginnie Mae mortgage-backed securities are sold to investors in the open market, which is called the "To-Be-Announced" (TBA) market. The current coupon of MBS is determined by the coupon rate of securities selling closest to the par value. The yield on the current coupon MBS is highly dependent on the prevailing market interest rates. In fact, the spread between the current coupon MBS yield and long-term yields such as the 10-year Treasury yield is often viewed as the risk premium of the MBS, which primarily compensates investors for prepayment risk and also

---

[51]The respective correlations are 0.06, 0.89, 0.81, and 0.98 for QE1, QE2, the Twist, and QE3.

for lower liquidity.[52]

As shown in Figure 4, the current coupon MBS yield and the 10-year Treasury yield are highly correlated ($r = 0.99$) except during QE1 ($r = 0.76$) when the market was still adjusting. The spread between the two was at a historic high of over 200 bps just prior to the start of QE1 because of the financial crisis and gradually settled into a 50 to 100 basis point difference, even during the between-QE periods.[53] The current coupon MBS yield averaged 3.30 percent during QE1 (with a standard deviation of 45 bps), 3.26 percent during QE2 (with a standard deviation of 26 bps), 1.85 percent during the Twist (with a standard deviation of 21 bps) and 2.88 percent during QE3 (with a standard deviation of 56 bps).

This section presented a discussion of how interest rates and mortgage rates have changed during the LSAP program and provided a context for how various macroeconomic and financial factors other than monetary policy affect them. The next section will describe the empirical approach to isolate and estimate the "stand-alone" effects of the LSAP program on long-term interest rates and then mortgage rates and discuss the findings.

IV Empirical approach

The last two sections demonstrated that the LSAP program has involved a variety of Fed strategies and that interest rates and mortgages rates have been affected by the LSAP program, as well as other macroeconomic and financial factors. The goal of this section is to develop an empirical approach to estimate the effect the Fed's LSAP program—particularly

---

[52]While the spread between the current coupon MBS yield and the 10-year Treasury yield is viewed as the risk premium required by the investors purchasing MBS, the spread between the MBS yield and the 30-year FRM rate is called the primary-secondary spread, or the premium charged by loan originators. This spread widened considerably prior to the LSAP program and has remained above its pre-LSAP spread. It should also be noted that the overall correlation between the current-coupon MBS yield and the 30-year FRM rate is quite high ($r = 0.90$).

[53]The current MBS spreads of 50 to 100 bps are lower than the historical long-term average of approximately 120 bps, a major accomplishment of the LSAP program.

---

tapering of the program—may have on mortgage rates. To accomplish that goal, this paper employs a two-pronged strategy. First, an event study is used to examine the market reaction to the past LSAP announcements and isolate the effect of the Fed's monetary policy on the 10-year U.S. Treasury yield from other events. Second, a dynamic time series approach is used to model the relationship between the 10-year Treasury yield and the 30-year FRM rate and show how mortgage rates have changed with interest rates. Then the two approaches are combined to test how a range of scenarios used as illustrative shocks on the 10-year U.S. Treasury yield from further unanticipated tapering of the LSAP program might influence mortgage rates.

IV.A An event study of public announcements during LSAP phases

This subsection presents an event study that shows how the 10-year Treasury yield reacted to various Fed announcement of the LSAP program, including the recent announcements of tapering. An event study methodology can quantify and test whether events, like public announcements, result in an unexpected change in a data series, such as the security price of a financial instrument. When measured over a short period of time, a change can be interpreted as an isolated reaction to an unexpected event. This section presents an event study of the effects of the LSAP public announcements on the yield of the 10-year Treasury Note. Market participants might react when the FOMC changes the LSAP program approach, the Fed chairman speaks about current economic conditions, or Federal Reserve Bank presidents opine about central bank policy decisions. The event study methodology has been employed by a number of recent studies of the LSAP program (Gagnon et al. 2011; Krishnamurthy & Vissing-Jorgensen 2011; Swanson 2011) as evaluated by Thornton (2013).

The event study technique relies on the assumption of an efficient market in which new information is reflected quickly in a price or valuation. Like a stock price, the Treasury yield is determined by the trading of highly liquid financial assets, Treasury Notes, and is hypothesized to reflect all relevant information. Any event that may affect their yield is expected to be priced in immediately because of ubiquitous news sources and computerized trading software.

IV.A.1. Event study methodology

Applying the event study methodology to the LSAP (or QE) policies involves analyzing changes in yields of Treasury bonds on dates when relevant information is released publicly. To conduct the event study, first, event dates are assembled based on when market participants become aware of the LSAP-related news or other announcements that could affect yields.[54] Then, as MacKinlay (1997) describes, the normal and abnormal changes are derived on those dates. [55] The normal change is defined as the expected change in yields if no event had occurred. The abnormal change is defined as the actual change less the normal change,

$$AR_t = R_t - E(R_t|X_t) \tag{1}$$

where AR_t is the abnormal change on date t, R is the change on date t, and $E(R_t|X_t)$ is the normal change on date t.[56] In other words, the normal change represents an estimate of what would have happened to the data series in question had no material news occurred

---

[54]Event dates are dates on which material information about LSAP policy becomes publicly known; dates on which, *a priori*, one would expect the market to react to LSAP policy news. In this case, event dates consist of dates on which official FOMC statements are released as well as dates on which former Chairman Bernanke discusses LSAP policies.

[55]In most event studies, the financial instruments in question are securities for which the relevant change in a given day is the return. For example, when analyzing a stock, a change in price from 20 dollars per share to 25 dollars per share represents a 25% return, and is equivalent to a move from 100 dollars to 125 dollars. As such, a typical event study uses terms such as "normal return" and "abnormal return." Because this study analyzes changes in treasury yields, the relevant metric is not the percentage change but rather the raw movement in yields. Consequently, the study will use "yield changes" or "changes" where many event studies would use "returns," except when using specific technical terms that use the word "returns" or where the use of "changes" could create confusion.

[56]Here, the conditional expectation is based on a constant mean return model, not a market return model. A variety of market return models were tried in an earlier draft of this paper. None performed as well as the constant mean return model. A constant mean return model is preferred in part because there is no single series that mimics or determines Treasury yields. In addition, series that predict the 10-year Treasury yield (such as the S&P 500 Index, a corporate bond index or an international bond index) are also affected by the LSAP announcements. See Appendix B for further details.

---

that day, and the abnormal change represents the change to the data series that one can attribute to events on that day.

Unlike other studies where events may be completely unanticipated, the events in this study are FOMC meeting dates and related announcements. The regular and preset dates allow market participants to develop a reasonable belief about when changes may take place and the expected effect of the announced changes. For that reason, this event study measures reactions when the Fed's announcement deviated from market expectations, which could be different from a counterfactual scenario where the Fed takes no action at all.[57] To the extent the market anticipated the Fed's announcement and had priced it in, the event study analysis should not indicate a statistically significant result on that particular date (assuming no other major news affects the Treasury yield). Related tests are performed to measure whether the news might have had an impact in the days leading up or immediately following the event.

For example, consider some key dates surrounding the end of QE1. On November 4, 2009, the Fed announced that it planned to stop purchasing agency debt and agency mortgage-backed securities by the end of the first quarter in 2010. On March 16, 2010, the last FOMC statement date before the end of the quarter, the Fed confirmed that it would stop purchasing said debt and securities by the end of the quarter. That day, the 10-year U.S. Treasury yield fell by 4.6 bps. On March 31, the last day of the quarter, it fell by 3.1 bps. Neither of these reactions shows the true effect of ending QE1 in March relative to not ending, because the market had already expected the Fed to stop QE1. Therefore, the interest rate changes on these dates represent not the effect of stopping QE1 compared to a counterfactual in which

---

[57]If the Fed were to indicate a regular decline in purchases by $10 billion, then continuing that behavior would be expected by the market and would not be expected to drive a significant result with this event study approach. However, there could be a non-zero and statistically significant reaction should the Fed choose not to decrease purchases, to double the amount, or to alter another aspect of the market (like short-term interest rates).

QE1 continues, but rather the effect compared to the previous market expectation.

As noted in Section II, the current LSAP phase, QE3, was announced on September 13, 2012, with no clear indication of the date it would end. The market, though, had formed an unobservable expectation about when and how QE3 would wind down. This expectation was further adjusted when the Fed started suggesting tapering in its announcements and speeches in mid-2013. By the time the Fed announced tapering on December 18, 2013, the market appeared to have had a near fully-formed expectation about tapering. Any similar future tapering that meets the market's expectations should result in modest effects.

IV.A.2. Event study results

Table 1 presents the estimated abnormal changes for FOMC event dates and speeches related to LSAP phases. The table describes each event and provides the 10-year Treasury yield prior to the event. The middle of the table shows the abnormal change on the event date, with significant results indicating an effect from the announcement. To understand whether the news might have been built into the days leading up to the announcement, the set of columns to its left provide cumulative abnormal changes for the 1 day, 2 days, and 5 days before the event date. These statistics could be significant if the market becomes aware of unexpected news just ahead of the announcement. To the right of the abnormal yield change is another set of columns for the cumulative abnormal changes after the event date for 1 day, 2 days, and 5 days. These last results could be significant if it takes an additional day or more to price in the effect of the unexpected news. However, changes that occur several days before or after an event have a weaker causal link with the event itself and are more likely to be polluted by other news affecting Treasury yields.

A detailed explanation of the specific event dates helps to clarify the expected and actual event study results further. While some of the event dates were only affected by the LSAP

Table 1: Event study results for FOMC dates and selected speeches during QE1, QE2, Twist, and QE3

Date	Period	Event description	Prior 10-year Treasury yield	Cumulative abnormal change before the event date			Abnormal change on the event date	Cumulative abnormal change after the event date		
				5 days	2 days	1 day	event date	1 day	2 days	5 days
11/25/2008	QE1	FOMC: QE1 Announced	3.32	-0.32**	0.31***	0.13*	-0.22***	-0.13*	-0.13	-0.44***
12/1/2008	QE1	Bernanke Speech: QE1 Explained Further	2.92	-0.28*	-0.06	-0.06	-0.19***	-0.06	-0.07	0.01
12/16/2008	QE1	FOMC: QE1 Affirmed	2.51	-0.23	-0.09	-0.06	-0.26***	-0.06	-0.18*	-0.08
1/28/2009	QE1	FOMC: QE1 Expansion to Treasury Securities Hinted	2.53	0.15	-0.09	-0.11	0.14*	0.19***	0.17*	0.27
3/18/2009	QE1	FOMC: QE1 Expanded	3.01	0.00	0.12	0.05	-0.47***	0.07	0.10	0.25
4/29/2009	QE1	FOMC	3.01	0.11	0.02	0.10	0.10	0.01	0.05	0.05
6/24/2009	QE1	FOMC	3.62	-0.04	-0.16	-0.06	0.06	-0.15**	-0.15	-0.15
8/12/2009	QE1	FOMC: Treasury Purchase End Date Announced	3.67	-0.02	-0.18*	-0.11	0.05	-0.12*	-0.15	-0.27
9/23/2009	QE1	FOMC: Agency Debt and MBS End Date Announced	3.44	-0.01	-0.02	-0.04	-0.03	-0.04	-0.10	-0.11
11/4/2009	QE1	FOMC: Agency Debt Amount Adjusted	3.47	0.02	0.08	0.05	0.06	0.00	-0.03	-0.04
12/16/2009	QE1	FOMC	3.59	0.21	0.04	0.04	0.01	-0.12	-0.06	0.15
1/27/2010	QE1	FOMC	3.62	-0.07	0.01	-0.01	0.03	-0.01	-0.06	0.06
3/16/2010	QE1	FOMC: Last FOMC Before QE1 End	3.69	-0.02	-0.03	-0.01	-0.05	-0.01	0.03	0.04
11/3/2010	QE2	FOMC: QE2 Announced	2.59	-0.05	-0.01	-0.04	-0.02	-0.08	-0.04	0.06
12/14/2010	QE2	FOMC	3.28	0.35**	0.07	-0.04	0.20***	0.06	-0.05	-0.17
1/26/2011	QE2	FOMC	3.33	-0.04	-0.08	-0.08	0.09	-0.03	-0.09	0.06
3/15/2011	QE2	FOMC	3.36	-0.16	0.00	-0.05	-0.05	-0.13*	-0.05	0.02
4/27/2011	QE2	FOMC	3.31	-0.06	-0.08	-0.06	0.05	-0.04	-0.07	-0.14
6/22/2011	QE2	FOMC: Last FOMC Before QE2 End	2.98	-0.11	0.04	0.03	0.00	-0.07	-0.12	0.13
9/21/2011	Twist	FOMC: Twist Started	1.94	-0.05	-0.11	-0.01	-0.08	-0.14*	-0.02	0.12
11/2/2011	Twist	FOMC	1.99	-0.12	-0.33***	-0.12*	0.00	0.09	0.05	-0.02
12/13/2011	Twist	FOMC	2.01	-0.03	0.04	-0.05	-0.05	-0.06	-0.06	-0.04
1/25/2012	Twist	FOMC	2.06	0.20	0.04	0.01	-0.07	-0.06	-0.10	-0.17
3/13/2012	Twist	FOMC	2.03	0.02	0.02	0.01	0.09	0.14*	0.15	0.23
4/25/2012	Twist	FOMC	1.97	-0.02	0.01	0.04	0.01	-0.05	-0.05	-0.06
6/20/2012	Twist	FOMC	1.62	-0.04	0.04	0.05	0.04	-0.04	0.02	-0.04
8/1/2012	Twist	FOMC	1.47	0.08	-0.08	-0.03	0.06	-0.05	0.04	0.13
9/13/2012	QE3	FOMC: QE3 (Agency MBS) Announced	1.76	0.16	0.10	0.06	-0.03	0.14*	0.12	0.04
10/24/2012	QE3	FOMC	1.76	0.04	-0.01	-0.06	0.03	0.03	-0.04	-0.10
12/12/2012	QE3	FOMC: QE Expanded to Treasury Securities	1.65	0.05	0.03	0.04	0.04	0.03	0.00	0.10
1/30/2013	QE3	FOMC	2.00	0.16	0.05	0.04	-0.01	-0.01	0.02	-0.03
3/20/2013	QE3	FOMC	1.90	-0.11	-0.09	-0.05	0.06	-0.05	-0.03	-0.11
5/1/2013	QE3	FOMC	1.67	-0.03	0.01	0.00	-0.04	0.00	0.11	0.14
5/22/2013	Tapering	Bernanke Speech: Tapering Suggested	1.93	-0.05	-0.02	-0.04	0.11	-0.02	-0.03	0.08
6/19/2013	Tapering	FOMC: Potential Tapering Mentioned	2.19	0.00	0.06	0.00	0.17**	0.06	0.18*	0.18
7/31/2013	Tapering	FOMC	2.61	0.11	0.05	0.01	-0.03	0.13*	0.02	0.02
9/18/2013	Tapering	FOMC	2.85	-0.12	-0.04	-0.02	-0.16**	0.06	0.05	-0.06
10/30/2013	Tapering	FOMC	2.50	-0.01	-0.01	-0.02	0.03	0.02	0.08	0.10
12/18/2013	Tapering	FOMC: Tapering	2.84	0.03	-0.03	-0.04	0.06	0.04	0.00	0.08
1/29/2014	Tapering	FOMC: Tapering	2.75	-0.08	0.03	0.00	-0.07	0.02	-0.03	-0.01

Notes: Table includes FOMC dates during LSAP programs. Changes in treasury yields are derived as the the difference between the yield at closing on the day of an event and the yield at closing on the day prior. Changes for 1, 2, and 5 days prior or after the event date do not include the change of the date itself. For example, the abnormal change on 11/25/2008 is the yield at closing on 11/25/2008 less the yield at closing on 11/24/2008. The cumulative abnormal change for the 5 days following the 11/25/2008 event date is the difference between the yield at closing on the fifth trading day after 11/25/2008 and the yield at closing on 11/25/2008 (not 11/24/2008). The cumulative abnormal change for the 5 days before the 11/25/2008 event date is the yield at closing on 11/24/2008 (not 11/25/2008) less the yield at closing 5 days prior. Significance levels are denoted as *** for 0.01, ** for 0.05, and * for 0.1.

announcements, there were dates that were also affected by other macroeconomic and financial factors and, at such times, the event study may not fully isolate the LSAP effects. A discussion of specific event dates is presented in Appendix B along with methodological details and explanations of results.

The event study suggests that on days when a major LSAP announcement was unexpected, the announcement had a dramatic effect on the 10-year U.S. Treasury yield. However, on days when the market had anticipated the policy announcement, the impact was muted. In general, the market was shocked dramatically during QE1 but the market reaction has become more measured over time; the effect of a LSAP announcement on the 10-year Treasury yield was much smaller in QE2 and QE3 than QE1. There are two reasons why this happened. First, the market had likely grown more comfortable with LSAP policies and had already built in the expected effect of the announcements after QE1. Second, the QE1 policies were "unprecedented" for the Fed but, in the time since, the market had become more adept at anticipating Fed decisions.[58] The lack of significant cumulative results for the shorter periods at the end of the event study sample suggests that the market had already priced in tapering. Prior to the Fed's announcement on December 18, 2013, earlier announcements had suggested tapering as shown by the large and statistically significant effect on June 19, 2013. Consequently, the effects will likely be small in magnitude from any further tapering news that conveys a continuation of the current Fed policy.

The results also suggest that, compared to QE1, the Fed has become clearer in communicating its intentions to the market and the market has become better at using macroeconomic data to anticipate what the Fed may do. The market was expecting the Fed's tapering in December when it began, and it correctly assumed that tapering would again continue in January. On these dates, the changes in 10-year Treasury yields were 6 and -7 bps, respec-

---

[58]See the Bloomberg article from March 18, 2009.

---

tively. With the economy on increasingly steady footing, the Fed had little reason to make a dramatic change, and the market had a good grasp of the Fed's intentions going forward. Given the steady course that the Fed has charted with tapering so far and the market's increasing ability to interpret macroeconomic data to anticipate Fed actions, these small effects are likely to continue with future tapering announcements.

However, when the market has been surprised by tapering news (e.g., June 19, 2013) or the lack thereof (e.g., September 18, 2013) the changes in 10-year Treasury yields have been large (17 and -16 bps for the examples, respectively). To the extent there are surprises in future LSAP policy announcements, these changes could indicate the possible magnitude of future effects. Moreover, when the Fed has completely shocked the market with its LSAP policies, it has moved the 10-year U.S. Treasury yield by as much as 50 bps. Indeed, the announcement of the expansion of QE1 on March 18, 2009 led to a 1 day drop of 47 bps. Tapering announcements so far have only slowed the rate of purchases. There is much greater uncertainty about if and when the Fed will start liquidating its current portfolio. Holding that portfolio still puts downward pressure on the market as former Chairman Bernanke laid out in the press conference on June 19, 2013. Although it is unlikely, if the Fed were to make a dramatic LSAP policy announcement, perhaps concerning its portfolio plans, the news could greatly affect the 10-year Treasury yields.

In short, the event study shows how the 10-year Treasury yield was affected by the LSAP announcements at discrete points in time. In the next section, a range of shocks to the 10-year Treasury yield (based on the varied magnitude of the event study results) will be used as scenarios to project the effects of such shocks on the 30-year FRM rate over a short continuous period. But the following section will start by describing the dynamic time series approach that models the relationship between the 10-year Treasury yield and the 30-year FRM rate.

IV.B   Time series estimations and projections

This subsection presents a dynamic time series model of how mortgage rates change with long-term interest rates. It provides insight on how the 30-year FRM rates changed with the 10-year Treasury yields during different phases of the LSAP program by comparing model projections with observed data. It also shows how a range of illustrative shocks on the 10-year Treasury Note from unanticipated events—as informed by the event study in the prior section—could affect the 30-year FRM rates in the near future.[59]

As part of the LSAP program, the Federal Reserve has bought agency MBS and agency debt, and bought and sold Treasury securities. The Fed cannot change long-term Treasury yields directly, but the event study in the previous section showed how the LSAP program affected Treasury yields and the effects manifested immediately with program announcements. As explained earlier in Section III, the 10-year Treasury yield is used as a benchmark for the 30-year FRM mortgage rate, i.e. any effect on the Treasury yields also affects mortgage rates. Therefore, the time series approach, as described below, models the relationship between the 10-year Treasury yield and the 30-year FRM rate. The extent to which the effect of the LSAP program announcements on the Treasury yields is reversed or becomes permanent goes beyond the scope of the event study in the previous section and the time-series model results are also constrained by this limitation.

A vector autoregression (VAR) model provides a formal technique where shocks to one

---

[59]In contrast, anticipated events would have no effect because they would be priced into the information sets used in the time series estimations. The Fed announcements in the middle of 2013 provide examples of unanticipated events: an FOMC announcement and a speech by former Chairman Bernanke included unexpected news about tapering the LSAP purchases. But by the time tapering was announced in December 2013 and the purchase reduction began in January 2014, the market had already priced in the effect of tapering from earlier anticipated events and the anticipated event of the tapering announcement, in effect, was already priced in. Therefore, if tapering continues as expected with $10 billion reductions per month in purchases, there will be no shock (due to an unanticipated event) because the policy is completely anticipated. But any unexpected events, such as even a mention of adjusting short-term rates in the March 19, 2014 FOMC meeting, could shock long-term interest rates and affect mortgage rates.

series can have dynamic short-run and long-run effects on one or more other series and such a model is used in this section to project the effects of changes in LSAP and Treasury yields on mortgage rates.[60] Formally, a VAR(1) model with a time-lag order one is written

$$\mathbf{r}_t = \phi + \mathbf{\Phi}\mathbf{r}_{t-1} + \epsilon_t \tag{2}$$

and provides an approach where $\mathbf{r}_t$ represents a multivariate vector of dimension k daily series, ϕ is a k-dimensional vector, $\mathbf{\Phi}$ is a $k \times k$ matrix, and ϵ_t is a sequence of serially uncorrelated random vectors with common mean, covariance matrix $\mathbf{\Sigma}$, and $i.i.d.$ normal over time.[61] The model is extended from 1 to p lags as

$$\mathbf{r}_t = \phi + \mathbf{\Phi_1}\mathbf{r}_{t-1} + \ldots + \mathbf{\Phi_p}\mathbf{r}_{t-p} + \epsilon_t. \tag{3}$$

For this paper, $k = 3$ since $\mathbf{r}_t = [\triangle\mathrm{Mtg}_t, \triangle\mathrm{Tsy}_t, \triangle\mathrm{LSAP}_t]$ and where Mtg_t stands for the 30-year FRM rate, Tsy_t represents the series of 10-year Treasury yield, and LSAP_t is the cumulative LSAP program purchases of agency debt, agency MBS, and U.S. Treasuries.[62]

The VAR analysis is broken down into two subsections. First, sets of in-sample projections during different periods of asset purchases are presented.[63] The sets are grouped by whether

---

[60]Event studies are based on the efficient market hypothesis in which assets follow a random walk. In contrast, the time series analysis allows for persistence in lagged multivariate series. To the extent that both Treasury yields and mortgage rates share a common stochastic trend, VAR models are useful for producing projections (as noted in Stock & Watson 1988).

[61]A theoretical and applied description of VAR models is presented in Section 8.2 of Tsay (2005). The book also covers VAR estimations, impulse response functions, and projections. Appendix C explains how these techniques are applied in this paper as well as the tests used to determine the appropriate estimation method, lag structure, and number of projected days shown in figures.

[62]Two of the daily series were downloaded on February 13, 2014 from Bloomberg using the tickers ILM3NAVG for Mtg_t (a daily series provided by Bankrate.com) and USGG10 for Tsy_t (constructed by Bloomberg from on-the-run Treasury indices). The other variable, LSAP_t, was formed from daily LSAP data on the Federal Reserve Bank of New York website. Bloomberg also provides series for the 1-year ARM (MTG_1YRARM, from the Freddie Mac U.S. Primary Mortgage Market Survey) and MBS current coupon rate (MTGEFNCL, from the Fannie Mae current coupon as generated by Bloomberg's mortgage current coupon note.) that are graphed earlier and used later for other projections.

[63]The LSAP program has not had a frequent or a large enough magnitude of asset sales to run that series separately or to split between asset types. Furthermore, while the different components of the cumulative

---

the projections start at the beginning or end of a LSAP phase. Projections from the beginning of a LSAP phase allow us to see if policies have been priced correctly into the observed values, which happens if projected and observed values remain very close; projections from the end of a LSAP phase indicate whether observed movements diverge as a LSAP program ends, or that a particular monetary approach only provided temporary stability from the effects of other market conditions.[64] Together, the two in-sample projections show how mortgage rates changed with interest rates during and after various LSAP program phases. Second, out-of-sample results are provided for the next quarter (65 business days) from the end of the full data sample.[65] Graphs show the immediate, short-run, and long-run responses of the 30-year FRM rates to illustrative shocks (separately on the 10-year Treasury yield and the cumulative LSAP purchase amounts). This exercise projects how a range of shocks to the 10-year Treasury Note, including an unanticipated tapering announcement (e.g. an abrupt end to the LSAP program), might affect the 30-year FRM rates.[66]

IV.B.1.   In-sample projections

In-sample projections provide a way to compare projected values with observed values.[67] Without such a comparison, it becomes difficult to judge how the modeling framework performs during particular LSAP phases and whether model projections are reasonable.[68]

---

purchases may have unique effects, their limited lifespans make it difficult for times series modeling.

[64]The start dates used for QE1, QE2, Twist, and QE3 are November 25, 2008, November 3, 2010, September 21, 2011, and September 13, 2012, respectively. The end dates are March 31, 2010, June 30, 2011, December 21, 2012, and February 12, 2014 (the end of the full data sample).

[65]February 12, 2014 is the end of the full data sample.

[66]Granger causality tests indicate no significant relationship between changes in cumulative LSAP purchases and changes in mortgage rates, in either direction. The results from this section hold, though, even if the VAR model is run with only two series, Treasury yields and mortgage rates. Such estimations show slightly larger gaps between projections and actual values with the in-sample projections and a wider projection spread under different shocks in the out-of-sample projections. A relatively small shock to Treasury yields, like +10 bps, still results in mortgage rates climbing to 5.0 percent. Two other series provided similar results and are presented in Figure 10 in Appendix D.

[67]Semantically, the term "in-sample" refers to periods where data are available to overlay on the projected series. The overlayed observations, though, are omitted from the estimation samples. Other researchers might refer to this approach as "out-of-sample" projections. The next subsection presents projections where data were not available for counterfactual comparisons and that approach is given the label of "out-of-sample".

[68]A better comparison than between the projected and observed values might be within the actual conditional VAR estimations before any projections are performed. In those models (as described later), the R^2

During several LSAP phases, the Federal Reserve has increased its purchase volumes while trying to provide clear announcements about its future activity. Both the Federal Reserve and the marketplace have had an ongoing learning process about how such changes are anticipated and priced into series. Thus, it is not unreasonable to expect projections to more closely resemble the actual observations during later LSAP phases.

Figures 5 and 6 depict the mapping from regression estimations (top graph for each phase) obtained from the time series model to projections in levels (bottom graph for each phase). The distinction between the two figures is that Figure 5 shows projections as if the data were cut off at the start of each phase while Figure 6 displays projections from the end of the phases. The graphs for each phase are presented with a top and bottom panel that represent the mapping described in Appendix C. The top panels show the projected values from the estimations of the first-differences along with their 95 percent confidence intervals (CI) as obtained directly from the time series model. The bottom panels show the reconstructed projected series and the observed values after applying a mapping algorithm.[69] Both panels share the same horizontal axis that shows the days after the phases began. Projections are constructed with a step of 65 business days, which equates roughly to 13 weeks or a quarter of a year. Almost no persistence is left in any of projections at the end of the time span.[70] This means all effects attributable to the beginning of the LSAP phases are temporary and they dissipate after sufficient time has passed.

Figure 5 contains projections that are computed at the *start* of each LSAP phase. All the projections are constructed without any data from during the phase. The top panel in the pair of charts for each LSAP phase depicts daily changes in the projections of the 30-year

---

values are nearly always at or above 0.90 and the numbers are reported in the figures' footnotes.

[69]Since LSAP had not begun at the start of QE1, the top left panels in Figure 5 reflect predictions and actual values of time series estimations for only Mtg_t and Tsy_t. The distinction is accentuated with an orange (instead of red) dotted line for the predictions. All other estimations also include $LSAP_t$.

[70]The length of the time span is affected by the chosen lag structure and is chosen specifically because little persistence remains after 65 days across any model.

Figure 5: 30-year FRM rate projections vs. actual trends from the *start* of LSAP phases

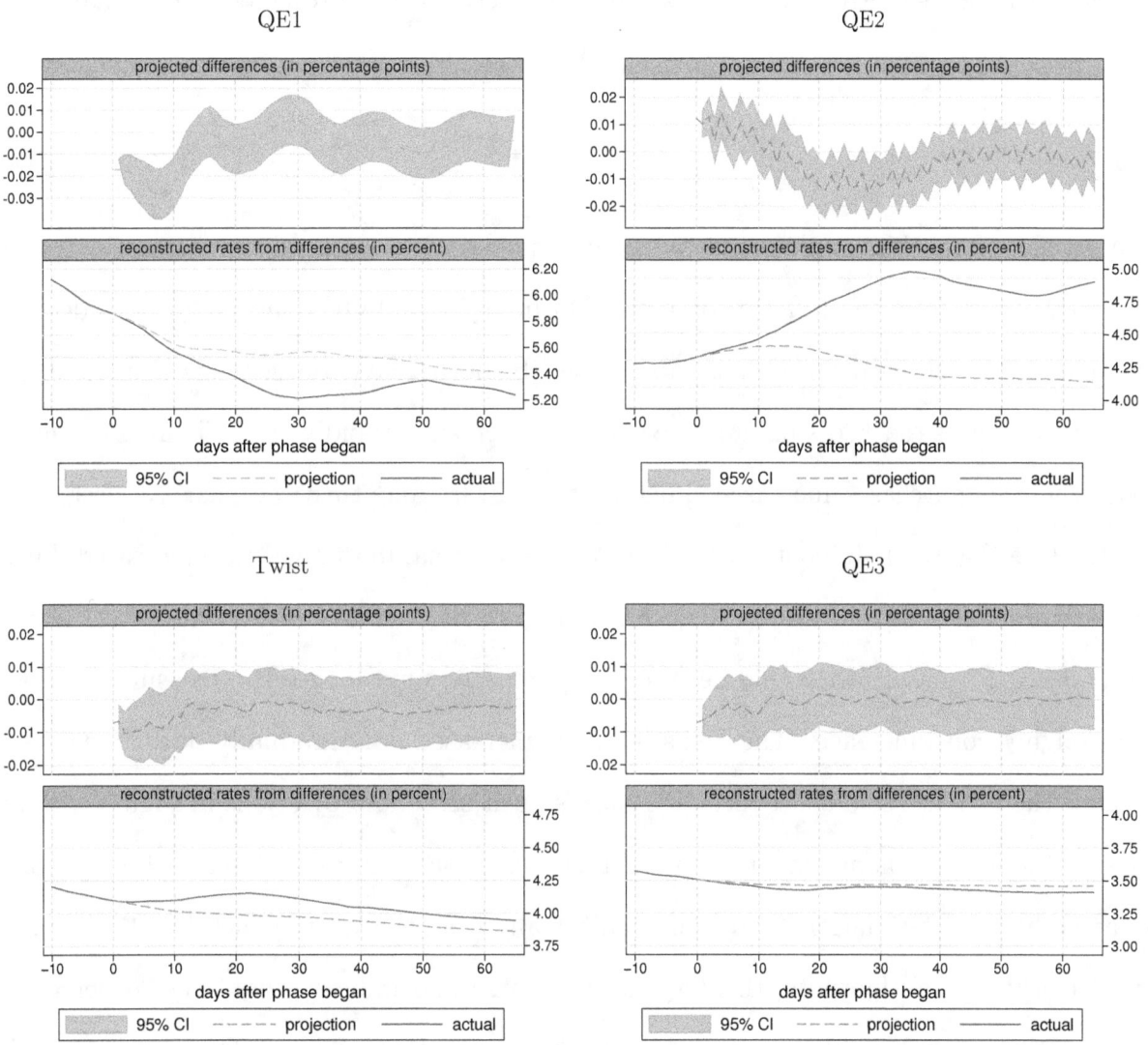

Source: Bloomberg. Projections from authors' calculations. Vertical axes show percentage levels and horizontal axes measure days. Conditional regressions are run leading up to day 0 (inclusive) and projections are used thereafter. The R^2 are high for each conditional VAR equation—QE1 has a fit of 0.92 for the Treasury series and 0.95 for the mortgage rate series; QE2 has 0.93 for Treasury, 0.93 for mortgage rates, and 0.95 for LSAP purchases; Twist has 0.93 for Treasury, 0.94 for mortgage rates, and 0.92 for LSAP purchases; and QE3 has values that round to one for each series.

FRM rate bounded by the 95 percent confidence interval. They depict the rate of change in the projections of the 30-year FRM rate from day to day in percentage terms. Negative values show that the daily percentage rates are falling. To facilitate interpretation, the bottom panel in each paired chart shows the difference between the projected and actual values of the 30-year FRM rate. This difference between the projected and actual values could be interpreted as the effect of each LSAP phase if no other factors had influenced the actual values.[71]

The graphs of the LSAP phases show various degrees of downward movement in the 30-year FRM rates from the LSAP program.[72] During QE1 and QE3, mortgage rates declined immediately but leveled off after a short time. In both LSAP phases, the Fed purchased agency MBS and the Fed's cumulative holdings increased rapidly (see Figure 2). During QE1, the Fed purchases increased quickly at the start and then fell sharply after a few months (see Figure 1). In contrast to QE1 and QE3, actual mortgages rate increased during the early days of QE2 and they only declined after a brief increase during the Twist. During the two LSAP phases in the middle, the Fed purchased only long-term Treasury securities at a roughly constant pace. The Fed's holdings increased only gradually during the Twist because the Fed also sold short-term Treasury securities. The projections in Figure 5 do not always start out or change in the same manner across the graphs of different LSAP phases because the VAR estimations were run conditionally from the start of each LSAP phase. As noted in the figure's footnote, the R^2 values are high and indicate that over 90 percent of the variation is explainable between the projected and actual values. The Twist and QE3 graphs show only small gaps between projected and actual series, which implies little effect

---

[71]Admittedly, such a comparison weakens as the phases become longer or major events take place. Also, the interpretations of the later phases cannot disentangle effects from prior LSAP phases; they could be thought of as a marginal influence of an additional LSAP phase because the series already incorporate the effects of prior LSAP phases.

[72]As noted in Section III, flight to quality and other factors also increased demand for Treasuries, drove up prices, and reduced yields during the LSAP phases. Since the Treasury yield is a benchmark for the 30-year FRM, similar behavior is observed in that series.

---

of the LSAP program during those phases.[73] Much of the LSAP policy was well announced and consistent across the two periods. QE1 and QE2 graphs, on the other hand, show larger gaps between projected and actual series. The higher level of projected series compared to the actual series during QE1 shows the effect of QE1 in lowering mortgage rates. QE1, when it was first implemented was quite novel and included many changes to the program during the early stage. The lower level of projected series compared to the actual series during QE2, in contrast, shows that QE2 was less effective than QE1 for two main reasons.[74] First, as shown in Figure 1, the lack of agency MBS purchases as well as the smaller overall size of purchases might have rendered QE2 weaker than QE1. Second, as noted in Section III, the strong stock market recovery at the start of QE2 might have offset at least some of the effects of QE2.[75]

Figure 6 illustrates projections that are computed at the *end* of each LSAP phase but the implications are slightly different from those in the prior figure. At the end of a phase, there is no continued promise of LSAP transactions. If the LSAP policy properly stabilized the market and was fully priced in by the end of phase, the projections, i.e. what might have happened if each LSAP phase had been allowed to continue, would be stable after the end of the phase. That appears to be true for all the LSAP phases.[76] Given stable projections, the difference between the projected and actual series can be interpreted in two ways. If no

---

[73]An alternate viewpoint might be that those periods had a significant effect that was priced into the market already before the start of the periods. Since the event study results in Table 1 do not indicate significant announcements prior to either period, that view extends beyond this study's framework but it remains possible that a long-run propensity effect could exist.

[74]Other events may have happened simultaneously in the first 65 days that are not being explicitly controlled for and those effects may not be incorporated into projections. Although VAR estimations are attractive for being simplistic yet powerful, the insights from comparing projected and observed values may be limited under such conditions.

[75]The stronger effects of QE1 compared to subsequent phases is also corroborated by the event study. As the Fed began to develop different LSAP phases, communication about the intent and the magnitude of the policy improved with each subsequent phase. This is evident in the smaller magnitude of effects and fewer statistically significant results in the event study, as well as the smaller gaps between the projected and actual values in the time series estimations of later LSAP phases.

[76]For QE3 projections, the model assumes that the last observable date in the data, February 12, 2014 is the end of the phase without any unanticipated announcements.

Figure 6: 30-year FRM rate projections vs. actual trends from the *end* of LSAP phases

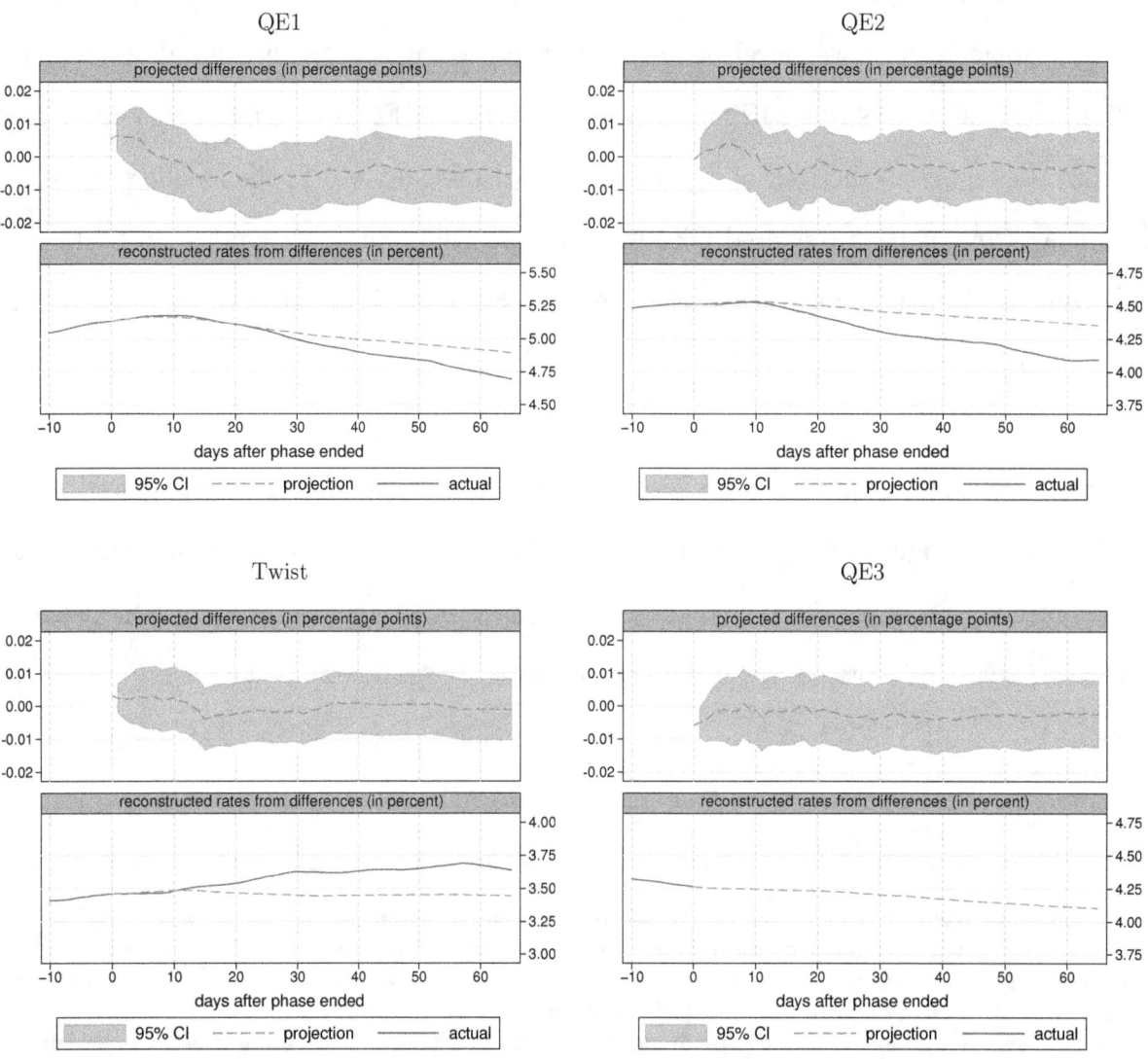

Source: Bloomberg. Projections from authors' calculations. Vertical axes show percentage levels and horizontal axes measure days. Conditional regressions are run leading up to day 0 (inclusive) and projections are used thereafter. The R^2 are high for each conditional VAR equation—the fit rounds to one for each series estimated at the end of QE1, QE2, and the Twist while QE3 has a fit of 0.92 for the Treasury series, 0.94 for the mortgage rate series, and 0.89 for the LSAP purchase series.

additional factors affected mortgage rates after the end of an LSAP phase and the end of the LSAP phase had little effect on the mortgage rates, then one might expect to see little divergence between the projections and actual values. Alternatively, the divergence between the two series would represent either the effect of ending the LSAP phase, an influence of other factors, or some combination of the two.

The data for QE1 and QE2 appear to favor the second interpretation. The decrease in actual rates were 20 to 25 bps below the projected values after each phase ended, suggesting that either the end of the LSAP phase, other factors, or a combination affected mortgage rates at that point. Section III discussed how other macroeconomic factors affected Treasury and mortgages rates after QE1 and QE2 ended.[77] The end of the Twist is somewhat different because the actual 30-year FRM rates increased while the time series relationship projected a flatter status quo. What also complicates the Twist phase is that it coincided with the early part of QE3 when the Fed shifted to increased purchases of MBS and Treasuries to support a stronger recovery. Unlike the QE1 and QE2 graphs, there is no clean break from the monetary treatment in place during the end of the Twist. For QE3, the time series model projected further lowering of the 30-year FRM rate. Therefore, results across all the LSAP phases suggest that, at least to some degree, the programs were already built into the market's expectations for four to five weeks (20 to 25 days) past the end of any phase. Afterwards, the removal of the LSAP treatment leads to a gap (of 25 bps) where the market has lower rates than is projected in QE1 and QE2 but higher rates during the Twist, most likely due to the effects of other macroeconomic factors.

Clearly, there is an important difference between tapering that reduces or temporarily stops monthly purchases and tapering that reduces cumulative holdings (i.e., the flow versus stock components mentioned in Section II.B). Until the latter occurs, monetary policy remains

---

[77]Figure 4 also showed earlier that the end of QE1 and QE2 was followed by sharp declines in Treasury yields and mortgage rates.

expansionary and it should not be a surprise when mortgage rates do not rise much even when purchases are reduced or temporarily stopped. Moreover, these in-sample projections were calculated without considering any additional shocks to U.S. Treasury yields or cumulative LSAP purchases from tapering decisions. Rather they were calculated simply based on the dynamic time series model of interest rates and mortgage rates that assumed no changes at the point when projections were computed. The next subsection explores how any shock scenario, including one from an unexpected tapering decision, might affect future values of mortgage rates.

IV.B.2. Out-of-sample projections

The figures in the last subsection showed that projections became closer to reflecting actual values in the later LSAP phases. This suggests that out-of-sample projections should perform reasonably well under a scenario without any shocks. However, shocks can be incorporated into projections to provide a range of expectations about how future policy changes might affect the 30-year fixed mortgage rate. Therefore the out-of-sample projections are timely because the Fed has now started tapering the LSAP purchases, but how and when the LSAP program ends—especially how and when the Fed will liquate its asset holdings—remains uncertain.

Figure 7 displays two rows with impulse response functions and projected shocks. The top row illustrates shocks to the 10-year Treasury yields while the bottom row illustrates shocks to the cumulative LSAP purchases. The left-hand side graphs have impulse response functions that indicate the immediate, short-run, and long-run responses to how a generic shock alters the 30-year FRM rate for a period out to 130 business days (or 6 months). The impulse response functions demonstrate how the 30-year FRM rate would respond to a one-unit change in the shocked variable.[78] The graphs on the right have projections under

---

[78]Recall that the VAR estimations are performed on first-differences (or the change from one day to the next). This does not mean, then, that the interpretation is as simple as an increase of 1.0% or 100 bps to

Figure 7: Out-of-sample 30-year FRM rate projections under two separate types of shocks

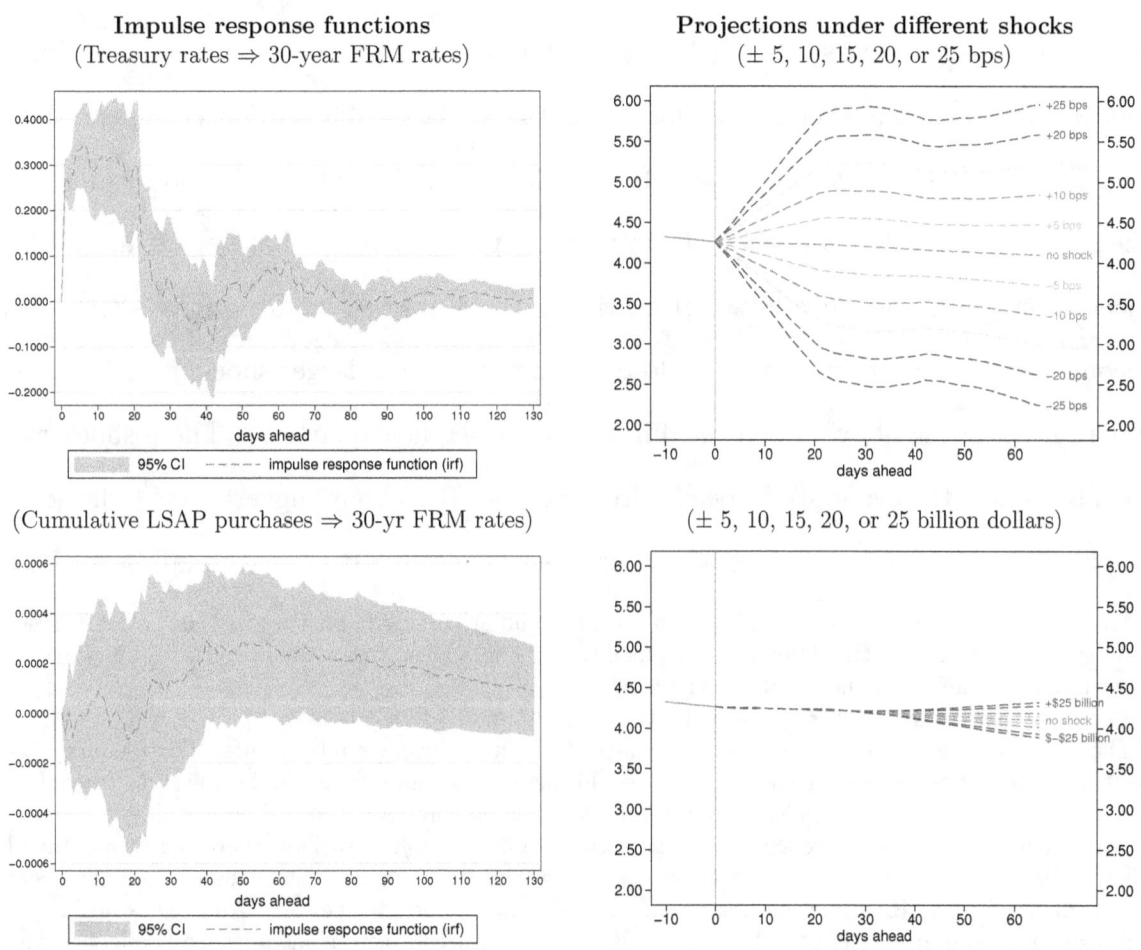

Source: Bloomberg and NY Fed. Projections from authors' calculations. Vertical axes show percentage levels and horizontal axes measure days. Conditional regressions are run leading up to the last trading date in the dataset and projections are used thereafter. The R^2 are high for each conditional VAR equation—the fit is 0.92 for the Treasury series, 0.94 for the mortgage rate series, and 0.89 for the LSAP purchase series.

different shock scenarios (in respective units of basis points and dollars).

As shown in Figure 7, a positive Treasury yield shock leads to an immediate and positive effect on the 30-year FRM rate that remains relatively high as it peaks after 5 days and begins to fall quickly after 20 business days. The effect switches briefly (for two weeks) to a negative response after 30 days, the response signal nearly vanishes after 65 days, and virtually no effect remains after 100 days.[79] The right graph incorporates these impulse responses under various shock scenarios ($\pm$ 5, 10, 15, 20, or 25 bps) where uncertainty in the 10-year Treasury interest rate can affect the 30-year FRM rate.[80] The no shock scenario is the same result as shown in the bottom right graph of Figure 6 that depicts an in-sample projection (without data overlayed) from the end of QE3. A small positive shock of +10 bps could push future mortgage rates close to 5 percent and a larger shock of +25 bps could result in them rising above 6 percent during the subsequent quarter.[81] These shock ranges are calibrated to the event study results from Section IV.A that suggest recent shocks have an average effect around 10 bps while earlier shocks (from QE1) tended to fall below 25 bps.

the Treasury yield or an increase of $1 billion to the cumulative LSAP purchases. The impulse response functions show a change in the differences. To facilitate the interpretations, the projections are shown back in percentage rate levels on the graphs to the right.

[79]Therefore, earlier graphs were projected out only to 65 days.

[80]The scenarios are based on prior shock magnitudes from the event study results. There is not a 1-to-1 impact where a 20 bps shock to Treasury yields would increase the mortgage rate by the same magnitude or proportion. Empirically, the impulse response function graphs show a one-unit increase does not have the same proportional effect on differences in mortgage rates. Those graphs also show there can be an immediate impact, a short-run change from a persistent effect, and a long-run (or permanent) change. All three aspects can be captured in a VAR estimation but not in a simpler event study framework. An event study measures a shock as an instantaneous effect while the VAR model captures both an instantaneous effect as well as an evolving effect over multiple periods. To the extent that a response function remains positive (as it does except for a small window between 30 and 45 days for shocks on Treasury yields), the positive responses continue to add onto prior values in a sequential manner and larger shocks will translate into greater future deviations, which is why the +25 bps shock widens much more than a +5 bps shock by the end of the projections. When the response function drops below zero then a positive shock sequence will converge back toward the "no shock" scenario. Hence, all the positive shock scenarios drop slightly between 30 and 45 days in the right panel but the negative response during those days is too small (compared to the prior and accumulated positive response) to transition the shock scenarios back to the "no shock" level.

[81]A single shock of +25 bps to the Treasury yield can also affect that series, as well. Indeed, the impulse response function of the Treasury on itself shows an immediate and strong short-term effect that fades out quickly after 20 days. Although the spread would grow between the 30-year FRM rate and 10-Year Treasury Note, the baseline would no longer be the lower unshocked level of Treasury yield or even its equivalent shift upwards of +25 bps because persistence would increase the series further.

In other words, should future tapering announcements by the Federal Reserve follow recent trends and result in an aggregate shock of +10 bps, the projections would suggest mortgage rates could rise to 5.0 percent by the middle of 2014. This level would represent a difference of close to 75 bps within a quarter from a scenario without a shock.[82] This magnitude is in the range of some of the larger changes in mortgage rates that were observed during the LSAP phases within one to five months after the Fed announcements. Hancock & Passmore (2011) has shown the two largest changes to be 64 bps and 82 bps.

Another insight from the out-of-sample projections involves the shocks to the cumulative LSAP purchases.[83] While the shocks to the 10-year Treasury yield above were informed by the event study model, the shocks to the cumulative LSAP purchases are intended to be purely illustrative. A positive shock to the cumulative LSAP purchase amounts leads to a quick but very mild negative effect on the 30-year FRM rate in the short term that switches to a mild positive effect around 25 days, then peaks around 50 days, and continues with a very moderate decay thereafter.[84] A permanent effect still remains at the end of the projection window but it is extremely small and appears to be diminishing over time. Thus, no matter how much cumulative LSAP purchases are shocked ($\pm$ 5, 10, 15, 20, or 25 billion dollars) there is very little response on the 30-year FRM as shown by the extremely tight scale (until 35 days) in the bottom graph compared to the projections presented above it.[85] This result suggests that the market appears not to react to the actual size of tapering. As described previously, despite the Fed's recent reductions of monthly purchases by $10 billion, the

---

[82]The estimate of approximately 75 bps is not an estimate of the spread between the U.S. Treasury Note yield and the 30-year FRM rate. In addition, this estimate does not imply an increase in the spread between the morgage rate and the Treasury Note yield.

[83]The ideal series to shock is the cumulative LSAP holdings of the Fed but that series is not available at the daily level. Therefore, this paper uses the cumulative LSAP purchases as a substitute.

[84]The cumulative LSAP purchases grows at a slower rate as purchases are tapered off. Therefore, the size of the positive shock illustrates different rates of tapering.

[85]As with the Treasury shocks, the impulse response function shows how the 30-year FRM rate responds immediately to a single shock to LSAP purchases and the persistence effect of the shock (i.e., whether it is permanent). The projected ranges incorporate the impulse response path under different shock magnitudes to show how rates might be affected.

outstanding holdings are still increasing and remain several hundred times greater than the current monthly purchase volume. Therefore, it is reasonable to expect that mortgage rates might not change further from the current level without a significant decrease in cumulative holdings.

IV.C   Discussion

In this paper, two econometric techniques provided an applied framework for studying the relationship between interest rates and mortgages rates and how the Fed's LSAP program has affected them. The study used the 10-year Treasury yield and the 30-year FRM rate to study the relationship between interest rates and mortgage rates. There were two main reasons for this selection: both are broadly representative of the market and the long-term relationship between the two has been historically tight. To some extent, the methodology in this paper can be applied to shorter-term interest rates and mortgage rates. However, the efficacy of the models will depend the strength of the relationship between the interest rates and the mortgage rates used. The 15-year FRM rate is highly correlated with the 30-year FRM rate and generally 50 to 100 basis points lower. It is expected to behave similarly to the 30-year FRM rate. The shorter term Treasury Notes, namely the 5-year and the 7-year notes, have lower yields than the 10-year note. However, the spread between the 10-year Treasury Note and shorter-term notes can change dramatically over time as reflected by the changes in the yield curve. Both the 30-year FRM and the 15-year FRM rates could also be potentially modeled with a combination of 10-year note with the 7-year or the 5-year note yields. In contrast, the short-term mortgages such as the 1-year ARM rate are related to short-term interest rates such as the 1-year Treasury yield or the LIBOR and the models might need some adjustments accordingly.

The empirical section performed three separate analyses. First, the event study showed how the 10-year Treasury yield changed after each key LSAP event, including the event dates related to tapering. Second, the time series estimations showed that daily 30-year FRM rates moved very closely with the 10-year Treasury yields and the in-sample model projections of the former were very close to actual values. The projections were within 25 bps up to a quarter later even though the model only included two other series, namely the 10-year Treasury yield and cumulative LSAP purchase amounts. The latter, however, appears to be more of an aid for refining estimates rather than a leading indicator of change. In contrast, the 10-year Treasury yield provides valuable information about how the 30-year FRM rate evolved and where it might be in the future. Third, the time series estimations also enabled out-of-sample projections to test the effects of a range of shocks on the 10-year Treasury yield on the 30-year FRM rate. The range of shocks were informed by the effects of LSAP announcements on the 10-year Treasury yield. This exercise illustrated how shocks to the 10-year Treasury yield, including those from unexpected events, could affect the 30-year FRM rate.

Finally, it should be noted that the LSAP program is still in progress and the true effects of the LSAP program will not be fully known until the program is completed. The last part of this study's sample overlaps with the beginning of Federal Reserve's tapering program. Data used in the paper ends on February 12, 2014. Tapering had been hinted at for over six months since May 2013 and there had been substantial speculation that some tapering action would be taken in the early part or middle of 2014. Tapering was finally announced at the end 2013 and began in 2014. But questions still remain about the frequency with which tapering will proceed, whether the tapering amounts will increase over time, and if it will continue at some point beyond just phasing out monthly purchases to include asset sales.[86] There is a big distinction between reducing the flow with purchase reduction versus reducing

---

[86]During the March 2014 FOMC meeting, Janet Yellen suggested that the Fed might begin using other policy tools, like increasing short-term interest rates, that could simultaneously affect Treasury yields and mortgage rates (see the FOMC press conference notes and interpretations by news sources like the *Washington Post* and *USA Today*). The 10-year Treasury yield rose 10 bps that day (from 2.68 on March 18 to 2.78 on March 19 per the Daily Treasury Yield Curve Rates released by the U.S. Department of the Treasury) after the unanticipated announcement.

the stock from asset sale. To this point, the LSAP actions so far have affected the Fed's holdings in only one direction and projections presented in this paper do not account for any reduction in the Fed's asset holdings. The true effects may also differ depending on the timing and the details of purchase reduction or net sales. While projections can be helpful indicators for policy makers and investors, their value depends on fully understanding the underlying assumptions used to arrive at them.

V Conclusion

In response to the Great Recession, the Fed was forced to depart from its traditional monetary policy techniques.[87] It purchased large amounts of agency debt, agency MBS and Treasury securities in four different phases (QE1, QE2, the Twist and QE3) over more than five years.

This study employed two econometric techniques to measure the effects of the current monetary policy on long-term interest rates and mortgages rate. First, the event study measured how key LSAP events, including tapering, affected the 10-year U.S. Treasury yield. Second, the dynamic time series regression provided a model of the 10-year Treasury yield and the 30-year FRM rate while also controlling for the cumulative LSAP purchase amounts. Third, the results from the event study were used to inform a range of shocks on the 10-year Treasury Note that could be used to test the effect on the 30-year FRM rate from any unanticipated event, including surprise changes to the tapering.

As intended, the LSAP program affected interest rates and mortgage rates. Indeed, mortgage rates were artificially lower than they would have been without the LSAP program and reached a historical low. The descriptive analysis discussed that long-term interest rates and mortgage rates changed during this time not only because of the LSAP program but also due

---

[87]Great Britain took similar actions around the same time. Japan, to some extent, has served as an early example because it began relying on quantitative easing to expand the monetary base in the early 2000s and was able to withdraw quickly in 2005 (see Wieland 2009).

---

to other macroeconomic and financial factors. Mortgage rates began resetting to a higher level when the Fed started suggesting tapering in mid-2013. By the time the Fed announced tapering at the end of 2013, mortgage rates had already adjusted to a higher level. An unexpected change to tapering could certainly result in higher mortgage rates. For example, a 10 basis point shock to the 10-year Treasury yield could increase the 30-year FRM rate further by about approximately 75 basis points over a quarter. Nevertheless, other factors, such as flight to quality and purchases of Treasuries by investors from overseas countries might also offset such increases. To be clear, this working paper is not predicting where mortgage rates will be in the near future. Rather, this paper informs how mortgage rates might change in the near future if only the effect of the LSAP program were to be measured, without consideration for any other macroeconomic and financial factors.

In conclusion, the U.S. monetary policy after the recent financial crisis—effectively the LSAP program—lowered long-term interest rates and mortgage rates by design. This policy played its intended role in stimulating the economy. However, when the Fed started suggesting tapering, the long-term interest rates and mortgages started resetting to levels higher than the LSAP-induced lower levels. By the time tapering was formally announced, the market appeared to have already adjusted for the tapering. However, any surprises about monetary policy, including but not limited to tapering, may further adjust mortgage rates upwards. In fact, shocks from other macroeconomic and financial factors could also lead to higher mortgage rates.

References

Aktas, N., de Bodt, E., & Cousin, J.-G. (2006). An empirical evaluation of accounting income numbers. *IAG School of Management, Universite cahtolique de Loubain, Belgium and ESA, Universite del Lille 2, France.*

Ball, R. & Brown, P. (1968). An empirical evaluation of accounting income numbers. *Journal of Accounting Research, 6,* 159–178.

Binder, J. J. (1998). The event study methodology since 1969. *Review of Quantitative Finance and Accounting, 11*, 111–137.

Brown, S. J. & Warner, J. B. (1980). Measuring security price performance. *Journal of Financial Economics, 8*, 205–258.

Brown, S. J. & Warner, J. B. (1985). Using daily stock returns. *Journal of Financial Economics, 14*, 3–31.

D'Amico, S., English, W., López-Salido, D., & Nelson, E. (2012). The Federal Reserve's large-scale asset purchase programmes: Rationale and effects. *The Economic Journal, 122*, F415–F446.

Fama, E. F. (1965). The behavior of stock-market prices. *The Journal of Business, 38*, 34–105.

Fama, E. F., Fisher, L., Jensen, M. C., & Roll, R. (1969). The adjustment of stock prices to new information. *International Economic Review, 10*, 1–21.

Federal Reserve Bank of New York (2013). Open market operations. From `http://www.newyorkfed.org/markets/openmarket.html`.

Federal Reserve Bank of St. Louis (2009). The financial crisis: A timeline of events and policy actions. From `http://timeline.stlouisfed.org/pdf/CrisisTimeline.pdf`.

Gagnon, J., Raskin, M., Remache, J., & Sack, B. (2011). Large-scale asset purchases by the Federal Reserve: Did they work? *Economic Policy Review, 17*, 41–59.

Hancock, D. & Passmore, W. (2011). Did the Federal Reserve's MBS purchase program lower mortgage rates? *Journal of Monetary Economics, 58*, 498–514.

Hancock, D. & Passmore, W. (2012). The Federal Reserve's portfolio and its effects on mortgage markets. Federal Reserve Board Working Paper 2012-22.

Krishnamurthy, A. & Vissing-Jorgensen, A. (2011). The effects of quantitative easing on interest rates: Channels and implications for policy. *Brookings Papers on Economic Activity*, 215–265.

MacKinlay, A. C. (1997). Event studies in economics and finance. *Journal of Economic Literature, 35*, 13–39.

Sirmans, C. S., Smith, S. D., & Sirmans, G. S. (2013). Determinants of mortgage interest rates: Treasuries versus swaps. *Journal of Real Estate Finance and Economics*. Forthcoming.

Stock, J. H. & Watson, M. W. (1988). Variable trends in economic time series. *Journal of Economic Perspectives, 2*, 147–174.

Swanson, E. T. (2011). Let's twist again: A high-frequency event-study analysis of Operation Twist and its implications for QE2. *Brookings Papers on Economic Activity*, 151–181.

Thornton, D. L. (2013). An evaluation of event-study evidence on the effectiveness of the FOMC's LSAP program: The reasonable person standard. Federal Reserve Bank of St. Louis Working Paper 2013-033A.

Tsay, R. S. (2005). *Analysis of Financial Time Series*. Wiley, 2nd ed.

Wieland, V. (2009). Quantitative easing: A rationale and some evidence from Japan. Tech. rep., NBER. Working Paper 15565.

Appendix A: The LSAP programs

This appendix describes each asset class that the Fed has purchased as part of the LSAP program in detail using the LSAP data through February 12, 2014.

Agency Debt

From December 2008 to March 2010, the Fed purchased $172 billion of agency debt at an average rate of about $10.8 billion per month. The actual monthly purchases ranged from $3 billion to $16.9 billion. Panel (a) of Figure 8 shows the details of the agency debt purchases with three panel groups.

First, as shown in the left panel group, the Fed purchased agency debt of Fannie Mae and Freddie Mac in equal parts (39 percent or $67 billion as noted on the top of the bars) and that of the Federal Home Loan Banks to a lesser degree (22 percent or $38 billion). Second, the middle panel group shows the distribution of the Fed's agency debt purchase by term to maturity. The Fed purchased debt with short to medium term to maturity. About 44 percent ($75 billion) of the debt purchased was set to mature in two to five years, 33 percent ($57 billion) in one to two years, and 22 percent ($38 billion) in five to ten years. Only about 1 percent of the debt purchased would mature in ten to 30 years. Third, the right panel group shows the distribution of the Fed's debt purchase by coupon rate. The Fed purchased similar share of higher-coupon and lower-coupon debt. A third of the purchases ($57 billion) had coupon rates of two to four percent and slightly more than a quarter of the purchases ($47 billion) had coupon rates of four to five percent. About a fifth of the purchases had coupon rates of five to eight percent ($36 billion) and another fifth of the purchases had coupon rates of two percent or below ($30 billion).

Agency MBS

During QE1, from December 2008 to March 2010, the Fed purchased $1.8 trillion of agency MBS at an average rate of about $120.6 billion per month. The actual monthly purchases ranged from $60.6 billion to $237.6 billion. After QE1 ended, from April to July 2010, the Fed purchased an additional $41.2 billion of agency MBS to reinvest principal prepayments from its MBS holdings at an average rate of $10.3 billion per month. While the reinvestment of principal prepayments from the Fed's MBS holding were diverted to U.S. Treasury securities starting in August 2010, they were again reinvested in agency MBS after October 2011. During the Twist period and prior to the start of QE3, the Fed reinvested $312.4 million of principal prepayments from its MBS holdings back into agency MBS at a monthly average rate of $28.4 million. During QE3, the Fed purchased an average of $57 billion of agency MBS per month. The actual purchase ranged from $54 billion to $95 billion per month with the target program purchase of $40 billion per month and the remainder as reinvestment of principal prepayments. By February 12, 2014, the Fed had purchased $1.4 trillion of agency MBS under QE3. The majority (55 percent) of MBS purchased by Feburary 12, 2014 was purchased during QE1, over a third (35 percent) during QE3 and a tenth during the Twist. Panel (b) of Figure 8 presents the details of the agency MBS purchases with, again, three panel groups.

The left panel group shows the agency distribution of the Fed's MBS purchases. The majority of the MBS purchased (60 percent or $2 trillion) was Fannie Mae MBS and more than a quarter (27 percent or $0.9 trillion) was Freddie Mac MBS. The remaining 12 percent ($0.4 trillion) was Ginnie Mae MBS. The Fed purchased a higher share of Fannie Mae MBS during QE1 (66 percent) than during the Twist (56 percent) or QE3 (52 percent), but the share of Freddie MBS was similar throughout the phases (27 to 29 percent). Consequently, the Fed purchased a higher share of Ginnie Mae MBS (21 percent) during QE3 than during QE1 (7 percent) or the Twist (11 percent).

The middle panel group presents the term distribution of the Fed's MBS purchases. About 92 percent ($3 trillion) of purchases were in 30-year MBS and 8 percent ($0.3 trillion) was of 15-year MBS. Nearly all the purchases (97 percent) during QE1 were 30-year MBS, the share of 30-year MBS went down to 90 percent during the Twist and further down to 83 percent during QE3. Consequently, the share of 15-year MBS increased from three percent during QE1 to 10 percent during the Twist and 178 percent during QE3. The Fed also purchased very small amounts of 20-year MBS during QE1.

The right panel group shows the coupon distribution of the Fed's MBS purchases. MBS purchases were evenly divided between the middle coupon groups: about 32 percent of the purchases were 3s and 3.5s, another 31 percent were 4s and 4.5s and about 28 percent were 5s and 5.5s—coming out to an even split of roughly $1 trillion each. Only a small share of purchases was in low or high coupon groups: 4 percent were 2s and 2.5s and 3 percent were 6s and 6.5s. In terms of timing, all of 5s, 5.5s, 6s, and 6.5s and almost all (83 percent) of 4s and 4.5s were purchased during QE1. Nearly all (93 percent) of 2s and 2.5s and almost three-quarters (76 percent) of 3s and 3.5s were purchased during QE3 with the remainder in the Twist.

U.S. Treasuries

During QE1, from March to October 2009, the Fed purchased $300 billion of U.S. Treasury securities at an average rate of about $37.5 billion per month. Actual monthly purchase ranged from $7.2 billion to $59.2 billion. Before QE2 began, starting August 17, 2010, principal prepayments from the Fed's MBS holdings were diverted to the purchase of U.S. Treasury securities. This reinvestment purchase continued until the Twist started on September 21, 2011. From August 17 to November 2, 2010 and from July 1 to September 20, 2011,

Figure 8: Distribution of purchases by the Federal Reserve

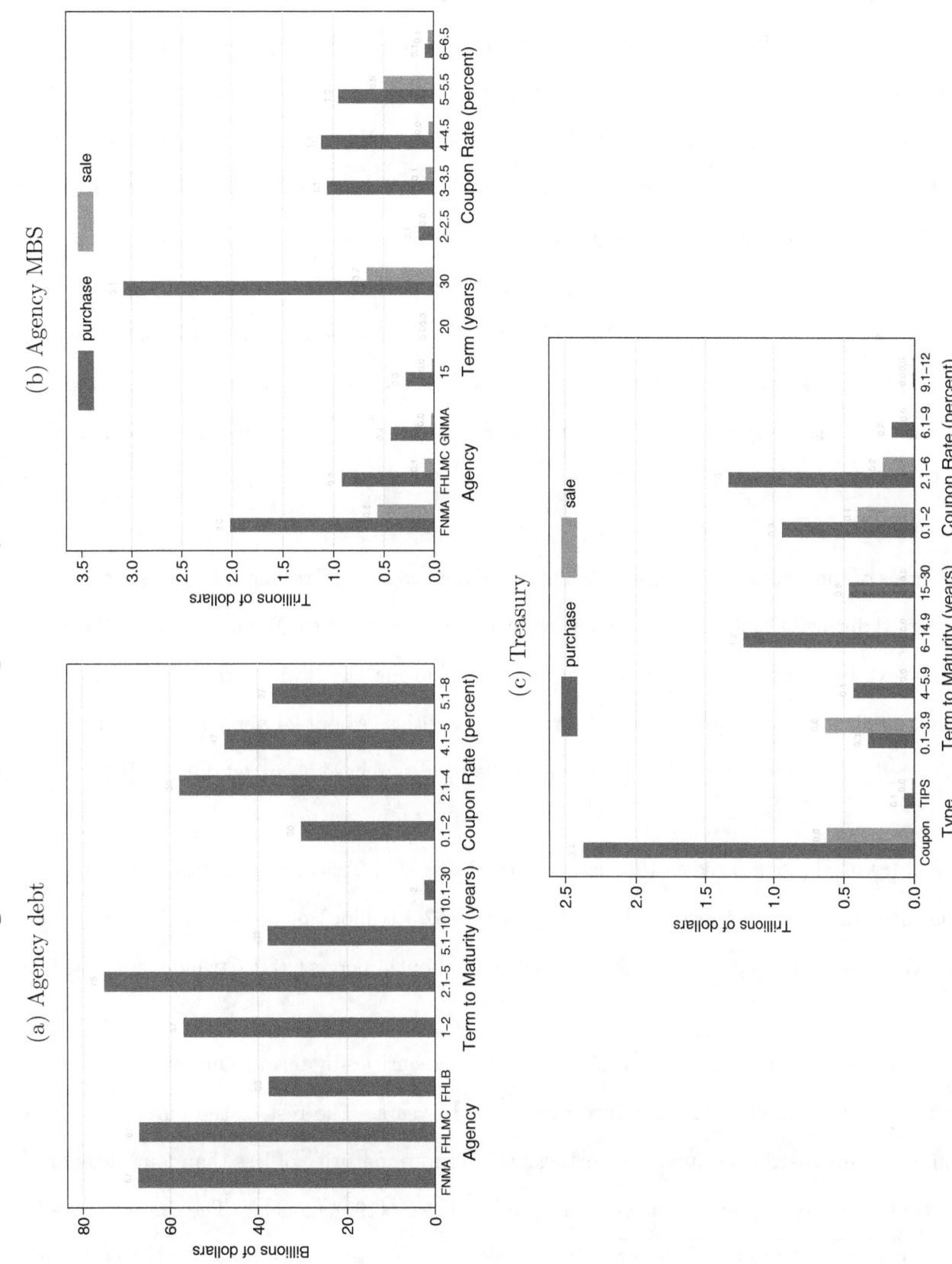

(a) Agency debt

(b) Agency MBS

(c) Treasury

Source: The Federal Reserve Bank of New York and Federal Reserve.

the Fed purchased about $103 billion of U.S. Treasury securities to reinvest the principal prepayments from its MBS holdings at the rate of roughly $13.1 billion per month. From November 3, 2010 to June 30, 2011, during QE 2, the Fed purchased about $778 of U.S. Treasury securities (approximately $97.3 billion per month on average) that included $600 billion in program purchase and roughly $178 billion in reinvestment purchase. During the Twist, from September 21, 2011 to December 31, 2012, the Fed purchased about $668 billion of U.S. Treasury securities with maturities of six to 30 years (at an average rate of $42.5 billion per month) and sold about $634 billion of U.S. Treasury securities with maturities of three months to three years. Finally, during QE3, from January 1, 2013, the Fed started purchasing U.S. Treasury securities at the rate of $45 billion per month totaling approximately $594 billion as of February 12, 2014.

In terms of the timing of purchases, 36 percent of the Fed's U.S. Treasury securities purchases occurred during QE2 (including the reinvestment purchase prior to QE2 and until the Twist). The next biggest purchase (27 percent) occurred during the Twist, which was offset by almost as big a sale of short-term U.S. Treasury securities. About 24 percent of the purchase occurred during QE3 and only 12 percent of the total purchase occurred during QE1.

Panel (c) of Figure 8 presents the details of the Fed's U.S. Treasury securities purchase. As shown in the left panel group, about 97 percent ($2.3 trillion) of the Fed's U.S. Treasury securities purchase consisted of coupons and only about 3 percent ($0.7 trillion) was TIPS.

The middle panel group presents the distribution of securities by term to maturity. One half of the purchases had term to maturity of six to 15 years. The rest of the purchases were almost evenly distributed among securities with term to maturity of less than four years (13 percent), four to six years (18 percent) and 15 to 30 years (19 percent).[88] The composition of

---

[88]It is not an error that there were more sales than purchases of short-term maturities. The Fed has always purchased U.S. Treasury securities and held nearly $0.5 trillion prior to the start of the LSAP program. The

purchase differed during the QE phases. The Fed did not purchase any securities with term to maturity less than four years during QE3. Over two-thirds of the securities purchased during the Twist had term to maturity from six to 15 years and a third had term to maturity from 15 to 30 years.

The right panel group shows the distribution of securities by coupon rate. Over half the securities purchased (55 percent or $1.3 trillion) had coupon rates of two to six percent and over a third (38 percent or $0.9 trillion) had coupon rates of two or below. Less than a tenth (7 percent or $0.2 trillion) had coupon rates of six to 12 percent. For timing, over half of the securities purchased during QE3 had coupon rates of two percent or below. In contrast, the majority of securities purchased during QE1, QE2 and the Twist had coupon rates of two to six percent.

---

sale of Treasury securities happened during the Twist when the Fed bought long-term securities and sold nearly the same amount of short-term securities. The remainder are dollar roll transactions.

Appendix B: Details on the event study

The basic applied approach to event studies began with Fama (1965), which addressed whether future or current stock prices are reflected in prior values. Methods were developed by Ball & Brown (1968) to study unexpected income changes and by Fama et al. (1969) to estimate how rapidly stock prices internalize new information in efficient markets. The techniques have been formalized in a more recent seminal paper to estimate the effect of specific events (like mergers and dissolutions) on the value of a firm (MacKinlay 1997). The techique was evaluated for its recent wide use in studies of monetary policy by Thornton (2013). The next several subsections describe the process of conducting the event study, graphical examples to highlight results, and a detailed explanation about specific event dates shown in this paper.

Selection of event dates

Event dates are selected based on being official FOMC statements and speeches by Fed representatives. The effect of such dates on Treasury yields can be given an expected direction based on the tenor of the news. In general, dates when the FOMC announces new LSAP policies or expansions of ongoing policies have a negative expected direction, because these actions would be expected to decrease Treasury yields. Announcements of tapering, end dates, or other reductions in LSAP policies have a positive expected direction, because these events are associated with increases in Treasury yields. Dates on which no new material information is provided have no hypothesized direction, and are not expected to be statistically significant. The creation or termination of an LSAP policy, if it had already been announced, is not expected to affect the change in Treasury yields. Finally, the change on an event date may not move in the expected direction if the news that was revealed was already anticipated by the market; similarly, there may be an unexpected reaction on dates when the FOMC does not pursue an anticipated course.

Normal changes

The normal change represents an assumption of how the 10-year U.S. Treasury yield would change if no event occurs. Often, when analyzing a stock, economists employ a market model, which predicts the return on the stock using the returns on an index, such as the S&P 500, as well as the return on similar companies. An alternative, the constant mean return model, assumes that on each day the normal return would have been the average return over a given period, called the estimation window.

A constant mean return model [89] is used in this paper. Unlike the securities that are usually the subject of an event study, changes in Treasury yields theoretically must have a true daily mean return equal to zero.[90] If the true average daily change of Treasury yields was non-zero, then multi-day yield changes with persistent positive (negative) changes would accumulate to higher (lower) levels. While non-zero mean changes can happen over a small sample of days, this does not take place on average over the entire sample period.

A constant mean return model is preferred to a market model in part because there is no single reference series that mimics or determines Treasury yields. In addition, many series that could be used to predict the 10-year U.S. Treasury yield, such as stocks, corporate bonds, and international bonds, are also affected by the QE announcements. Using any of these series to predict the 10-year U.S. Treasury results in endogeneity issues and systematic misestimation of the effect of the LSAP announcement.[91]

---

[89]Technically, the model is not using returns, as noted above, and is instead using changes in the treasury yield, so it could be called a "constant mean change model." However, the traditional term is used to avoid confusion about the methodology.

[90]The mean change is nearly zero for the estimation window—it has a 1 day mean return of -0.4 bps (with standard error of 0.5 bps)

[91]For example, consider a hypothetical day on which an LSAP announcement is made and the 10-year U.S. Treasury yields fall by 20 bps. The announcement and subsequent drop in yields makes U.S. Treasury Notes less desirable, causing investors to buy international bonds, so their yields decrease by an average of 10 bps. In reality, the effect of the LSAP announcement on the 10-year U.S. Treasury was a 20 bps shock, but a model that uses international yields to predict the 10-year U.S. Treasury yield would attribute some of that shock to the change in international yields and, consequently, underestimate the effect of the announcement.

Estimation window

The estimation window is a sample period used to estimate characteristics of a data series.[92] In this paper, the window measures the standard deviation of changes in the 10-year U.S. Treasury yield. In general, the estimation window should be similar to the event period and it is often chosen to directly precede the event while avoiding any overlap (as noted in MacKinlay 1997). There is no set length, though, for an estimation window. A year, or 250 trading days, is a common estimation window length when dealing with daily data (MacKinlay 1997; Binder 1998; Aktas et al. 2006). This event study uses a 261 day estimation window from June 30, 2007 through June 30, 2008. This estimation window captures volatility associated with the financial crisis (assuming it will continue during the analysis period) and ends as rumors began about the FOMC increasing its asset purchases. Several other estimation windows were tested with little tangible difference to the results.[93]

Methodology

To estimate the common mean return model, the abnormal change is calculated as the change in U.S. Treasury yield over the event window [94] and the standard deviation is drawn from the daily changes in the estimation window. For a single event date, the test statistic reduces to the ratio of the abnormal yield change and its standard error, or $t = AR/s$, where AR represents the abnormal yield change and s is the estimation window's standard deviation (following the work of Brown & Warner 1980, 1985). In addition, t-statistics are generated for the 1, 2, and 5 day periods following and preceding events as $t = \frac{\sum AR/N}{s/\sqrt{N}}$, where N is the number of days in the period (1, 2, or 5) and the standard deviation calculated over the

---

Indirectly, though, it was the announcement that drove the change in international yields. Several market models were tested, including those utilizing domestic corporate bonds, international government bonds, and stock indices, but the constant mean return was deemed most appropriate for the U.S. Treasury yield.

[92]From an experimental standpoint, the estimation window could be thought of as the control and the event dates are the treatments being applied at different times.

[93]Models were run using an estimation window from June 30, 2000 through June 30, 2008, from January 1, 2002 through December 31, 2002, as well as an in-sample estimation window (with event dates removed). None of these alternative estimation windows altered the results in a material way.

[94]as noted above, the normal change is assigned to be zero.

---

daily changes in the estimation window.

A detailed explanation about specific event dates

The result for an event date can sometimes be obvious and expected. However, there are dates when there might be an ambiguous hypothesis or when several other factors could influence the magnitude of an announcement. The following text provides a detailed explanation about specific event dates.

On the first date in the event study, November 25, 2008, the Fed announced that it would purchase agency debt as well as mortgage backed securities. In addition, though, the Commerce Department released a report with negative news about the economy. That day, the 10-year U.S. Treasury yield fell by 22 bps. Bloomberg news reporters attributed the changes to both the Fed announcement and the macroeconomic news, writing stories about how "U.S. Treasuries gain as GDP shrinks most since 2001 recession" and "Treasuries rally as Fed plan to buy mortgages prompts hedging."[95] These headlines suggest that the LSAP news on that day played a role in the decline of the Treasury yield, but that the full 22 bp decrease should not be attributed solely to it. Throughout the event study, on any day where there is other news moving the Treasury yield in the same direction as the LSAP event, the full change should not be attributed to the event.

However, there are other event days on which there was a stronger link between the change in the Treasury yield and the event. For example, consider the biggest shock, on March 18, 2009, when the Fed first announced it would buy Treasury notes as part of QE. Leading up to the announcement, the market did not anticipate the Fed buying exceptional quantities of government debt. Beforehand, Bloomberg news reported that strategists at Goldman Sachs, UBS Securities LLC, RBS Greenwich and Banc of America Securities-Merrill Lynch,

---

[95]See the Bloomberg article from November, 25, 2008.

---

and at Jefferies Group, Newedge USA and MF Global Ltd., all believed that central bank policymakers would not announce a plan to purchase U.S. debt.[96] The Fed proved them wrong by announcing it would buy up to $300 billion of Treasuries. By the end of the day, the 10-year U.S. Treasury yield had fallen 47 bps from the day prior. Market commentators attributed the drop to the market surprise after the Fed's announcement, "Treasury 10-year note yields fell the most since 1962 as the Federal Reserve surprised investors with plans to purchase as much as $300 billion in government debt."[97] Ajay Rajadhyaksha, the head of fixed-income strategy at Barclays Capital in New York described the day in the following way, "[The FOMC] wanted to shock the market and they succeeded."[98] Thus, March 18, 2009 demonstrates how a large shock to the 10-year U.S. Treasury yield occurred when the market was surprised by major LSAP policy announcements.

In contrast to the two event dates describe above, the Fed has made major announcements that have had no tangible effects on the 10-year Treasury yield. For example, consider the day that QE3 was announced, September 12, 2012. Leading into the Fed's speech, Bloomberg news reported that the Fed was projected to announce a third round of bond purchases and that Bank of America suggested that Bond-market yields had "largely priced-in" expectations.[99] During the day, Treasury yields actually decreased leading up to the announcement.[100] After the announcement, yields rose and finished the day down 3 bps, which corroborates reports about how the market was disappointed with the news. Still, the cumulative abnormal return suggests no statistically significant impact measured at 1 day, 2 days, or 5 days around the event. This day illustrates that when the market anticipates an LSAP policy change, the effect on Treasury yields can be muted—even with an announcement of a new QE.

---

[96]See the Bloomberg article from March 18, 2009.

[97]See the Bloomberg article from March 18, 2009.

[98]See the Bloomberg article from March 18, 2009.

[99]See the Bloomberg article from September 13, 2012.

[100]See the Bloomberg article from September 13, 2012.

Bernanke first mentioned slowing or stopping QE3 to Congress on May 22, 2013. Following his testimony, Bernanke answered a question about potential reduction of QE3 purchases by saying: "If we see continued improvement and we have confidence that that's going to be sustained then we could in the next few meetings ...take a step down in our pace of purchases".[101] The 10-year Treasury yield increased by 11 bps on that day, and Bloomberg attributed the change to Bernanke's comments with the headline "U.S. 10-year yield tops 2% as Bernanke says Fed may taper buys." The article quoted Christopher Sullivan as remarking, "The market seized upon the bit of the Q&A exchange about the anticipated timeframe about an adjustment to QE." However, the increase was relatively small because the statement was much less concrete than remarks that have driven larger changes.

Leading up to the next FOMC announcement on June 19, 2013, the market was speculating about potential tapering announcements.[102] That day, the official FOMC statement was very similar to the previous month's statement. However, in the press conference, former Chairman Bernanke indicated that if the economy recovered in a manner consistent with the FOMC's projections, the Fed would begin moderating purchases later in the year and finish around the middle of 2014. Those remarks were the first time that the former Chairman had suggested potential dates for when the FOMC believed tapering might start. He repeatedly emphasized, however, that the plan was subject to the economic data; if the economy performed better or worse than the FOMC's projections then purchases would slow more or less quickly than he had outlined. During that day, the 10-year Treasury yield increased 17 bps. Bloomberg news attributed the increase to the announcement, writing, "Ten-year yields climbed to a 15-month high after Bernanke said policy makers may 'moderate' their $85 billion in monthly bond purchases later this year and may end them around mid-2014 if economic growth is consistent with their forecasts." The 17 bp jump on June 19 could be attributed to the market anticipating tapering sooner than it had previously imagined.

---

[101]See the Reuters article from May 22, 2013.
[102]See the Bloomberg article from June 18, 2013.

In the following months, market participants tried to be the first to anticipate the Fed's actions surrounding tapering. As Jason Rogan told Bloomberg news on September 13, 2013, "People are trying to be a bit nimble in front of the Fed. There's a lot of cash on the sidelines."[103] That day, Bloomberg reported in the same article that, in a survey of 34 economists, the median expectation was that at the upcoming meeting monthly purchases of Treasuries would be reduced from $45 billion to $35 billion. Before the Fed's announcement on September 18, a Bloomberg survey of 64 economists revealed the majority still expected tapering of $5–20 billion per month for Treasuries and/or $5–10 billion per month for MBS purchases.[104] However, the Fed made no such announcement, and the 10-year Treasury yield fell on the day by 16 bps. Bloomberg attributed the change to the market's disappointment in the announcement, writing "Treasuries and gold rallied as the Federal Reserve unexpectedly refrained from reducing its monetary stimulus."[105] With this event date, the lack of a change in LSAP policies could itself be a significant event if the market believed that there would be a shift but no change actually took place.

The first actual tapering announcement occurred at the next FOMC meeting on December 18, 2013. The market had been anticipating tapering for months, although there were some mixed opinions about whether or not the Fed would taper.[106] The Fed announced it would reduce monthly LSAP purchases by $10 billion. That day, the 10-year Treasury yield increased by only 6 bps. After the announcement, Bloomberg quoted an institutional investor in fixed income securities as saying, "It seemed inevitable, and it was time to pull the trigger. The market was prepared for it. [Tapering] is going to be slow, relatively measured, and contingent on their forecasts."[107] Because the market anticipated the tapering announcement, the shock was relatively muted, and the yield change was insignificant.

---

[103]See the Bloomberg article from September 13, 2013.

[104]See the Bloomberg article from September 13, 2013.

[105]See the Bloomberg article from September 18, 2013.

[106]This was cited in the Bloomberg research roundup from December 18, 2013.

[107]See the Bloomberg article from December 18, 2013.

On January 29, 2014 the Fed continued to taper by reducing its purchases a further $10 billion. That day, though, had other confounding news. Bloomberg news reported that, "Treasury 10-year note yields fell to the lowest level in two months as investors sought a haven from emerging-market turmoil even with the Federal Reserve forecast to announce a second reduction in its bond-buying program."[108] A Bloomberg survey of economists actually predicted the $10 billion reduction in purchases before the announcement. Investor concern about emerging markets caused a flight to quality, increasing Treasury demand and pressuring yields downward.a

---

[108]See the Bloomberg article from January 29, 2014.

Appendix C: Details on the time series modeling

The text describes the dynamic time series modeling while avoiding some details. This section offers that information.

VAR estimations are performed with all variables being first-differences of the daily smoothed levels.[109] First-differences help solve two issues: non-stationarity and the effects of the shocks. Daily mortgage and Treasury rates are likely to share significant negative correlations with the cumulative asset purchases as shown in Section III. Also, the daily mortgage and Treasury rates are correlated with each other because they both suffer similarly from shocks, such as decisions made by the Federal Reserve. First-differencing reduces such correlations and diagnostic tests do not indicate problems of non-stationarity. A time-lag order of 25 days was chosen based on partial autocorrelations and Lagrange multiplier tests on the residuals.[110] First-differencing also provides an easier visual interpretation of shocks. When graphing a projection of differences or an impulse response function, the immediate effect can be shown when a series starts either above or below zero (or quickly moves away, showing an

---

[109]A variable's first-difference is its value change from the prior day to the current day. Smoothing (1, 2, 3, 4-week moving averages with equal weights and centered windows) allows us to reduce volatility. Given that results are similar across smoothing windows, a 4-week moving average was applied to resemble ongoing smoothing methods used by the Federal Reserve (see papers by Hancock & Passmore (2011, 2012)).

[110]No contemporaneous effects are anticipated but the VAR model is violated if the series are cointegrated, which exists if Equation 3's sequence of random vectors ϵ_t are correlated with each other. Depending on the lag structure and whether only Tsy_t or LSAP_t are estimated with LSAP_t, there is some evidence of cointegration of rank 1. As a result, estimations were run with a VECM approach but the projected results are nearly identical between the VARs and VECMs. This is likely because VARs are already being run in first-differences to avoid concerns of non-stationarity. VARs are used for simplicity. The overall results do not change drastically, either, if the lag structure is reduced to 20 days or increased to 30 days. Finally, at the conclusion of this study, we were introduced to recent work that suggests the 10-year Treasury might be outperformed by the 10-year Treasury swap in estimations of mortgage rates (Sirmans et al. 2013). A comparison between those variables shows the results are very similar, with a log-likelihood of 10,336 for the 10-year Treasury yields versus 10,388 for the 10-year Treasury swap rate. The R^2 values are close for VAR estimations over the whole sample—estimations with the 10-year Treasury yields series have values of 0.92 for the Treasury yield, 0.94 for the mortgage rate, and 0.89 for the LSAP purchases; in contrast, estimations with the 10-year Treasury swap rate series have values of 0.93 for the swap rate, 0.93 for the mortgage rate, and 0.90 for the LSAP purchases. The 10-year Treasury yield estimations explain more variation in the mortgage rate series (a goal of this paper is to model it well) but there is almost no tradeoff between rates and swaps.

"immediate" response in the early periods). A lack of long-term persistence is clear when a response converges to zero with time, which denotes that no further changes are left from the initial impulse. Interpreting differences and impulses is straightforward because the reference is a change away from zero instead of a particular index level.

The projections can be performed in levels or differences with data available until a particular point in time (like the start or end of a LSAP phase). Projections of levels are directly comparable to observed values. Projections of differences, though, show the change in levels from a prior period. A recursive process can map these projections back into levels in the following manner:

1. Let there be an observed series (i) with projected values (called f) which come from a VAR estimation of first-differenced values of it along with other series up to a particular period (t). Projections begin after t and are part of an arithmetic sequence.

2. Define the projected level variable $\tilde{i}$ as beginning in time period t and missing beforehand. The projected series initializes with the observed series's value in t, or $\tilde{i}_t = i_t$.

3. For the first time period with projections, the projected variable is the summation of the prior observed value and the first-differenced estimate, or $\tilde{i}_{t+1} = i_t + f_{t+1} = \tilde{i}_t + f_{t+1}$.

4. The projected variable is, in all subsequent periods, a recursive evolution of the prior projected variable and the current projection value, or $\tilde{i}_{t+n} = \tilde{i}_{t+(n-1)} + f_{t+n} = i_t + \sum_{j=1}^{n} f_{t+j}$ for a projection out to n steps.

All projections are computed without using any data from that LSAP phase, which means the overlay between projections and observed values provides a kind of hypothetical or counterfactual scenario for what might have happened in the absence of each QE phase or any other outside influences. The previously mentioned steps are used to reconstruct levels (bottom panels) based on projections of first-differences (top panels).

In-sample projections

For the projections computed at the start of each LSAP phase, all of the first differences have an immediate effect (positive in QE2 but negative in QE1, the Twist, and QE3) that becomes smaller in the short-run and disappears in the long-run (meaning there is no permanent effect in differences). QE2 is slightly different in that the projection starts above zero, values become negative in the third week, and then the series converges toward zero over time (although there may be a slightly negative and permanent effect).[111] These movements in the differences are captured in the projected values shown in the bottom panels. For the Twist and QE3, the immediate negative effects translate to falling projected values (dotted red line) that drop at a faster rate than the actual values (solid blue lines) in the first few days after those phases began. The small positive difference in QE2 is shown when the projected values reach an inflection and begin to decrease around 10 business days after the phase began and continue until the differences fall close to zero around 40 days when the reconstructed levels begin to flatten out. The QE2 phase poses a challenge for projecting beyond the first month (or 20 business days) with the likely culprit being a change in LSAP policy. During QE2, the Federal Reserve channeled its purchases to Treasury securities (there were no sales or any activity in Agency MBS or debt) and did so at double the magnitudes as experienced in QE1.

Figure 1 showed earlier that policies became more stable (i.e. monthly purchases and sales remained rather constant) during the Twist and QE3 phases, hence the tighter bands between the projections and actual series during those phases. After a full quarter into the phase, projections were more than 65 bps below actual values in QE2 but the gap was a mere 10 bps for the Twist and QE3 phases. Overall, the projected and actual values are quite good

---

[111]The period is notable for another reason. If VARs are run on only Treasury and mortgage rates, the projected results are quite similar to what is shown in Figure 5 but there is much less volatility during QE2. This is consistent with the earlier idea that the Fed improved its signals and the market improved its pricing in later LSAP phases.

(with differences under 10 bps for the Twist and QE3) considering they go out 65 steps and only involve three series, Mtg_t, Tsy_t, and $LSAP_t$. With LSAP policies becoming transparent through the Twist and QE3, there seemed to be fewer surprises—projections came close to actual values because information on future anticipated changes had been internalized well into the series.

For the projections computed at the end of each LSAP phase, the difference between the projected and actual values is also relatively small (never exceeding 25 bps by the next quarter). The projection for QE3 is not overlayed with actual data because it was performed at the end of the sample dataset. Projections match actual values for the first 20 to 25 business days (or four to five weeks) after the phases end but then the actual values drop much more than the projections during QE1 and QE2. Projections remain stable while rates rise after the end of the Twist.[112] The QE3 phase graphs lack actual values because they are out-of-sample predictions from where the data feed stops after February 12, 2014. Interestingly, the rates stay stable for the next 20 business days and begin to fall after 30 business days (six calendar weeks) to 4.15%. A similar set of predictions had been run in an earlier version of this paper where the data ended on December 16, 2013 (two days before the official tapering announcement) and the projected rates had increased from around 4.5% to 4.6% then fell back to 4.5%. Under both out-of-sample exercises, the magnitude of the drops are about the same from 20 business days to the end of the projected series but the projections presented for QE3 in Figure 6 do not show rising mortgage rates. A possible reason is that tapering has only recently begun and, although monthly purchases are being pulled back, cumulative holdings continue to grow.

---

[112]A closer match between actual and projected values (a difference of only 5 bps more than a quarter later) is found if the Twist's "end" date is defined as when it was supposed to end (June 30, 2012) instead of its actual termination (December 31, 2012). The actual termination is shown in Figure 6.

Out-of-sample projections

A VAR approach is not just useful for constructing in-sample comparisons of how projections compare to actual values. When the projections are closely related to the actual values, it might also make sense to turn to out-of-sample projections where projections can provide an idea of how series might evolve in the near future.[113] An out-of-sample projection can be constructed under several hypothesized shock scenarios, too, to test how series might react to unanticipated events. To begin a shock scenario, an assumption is made: persistence evolves per the same VAR parameter estimates as a scenario without shocks. Although this means that impulse response functions will be the same regardless of the shock size, it still allows for unequal shock magnitudes to result in unique series of future projected levels. When reconstructing a projection, as done earlier, a VAR estimation is performed up to a particular period. For simplicity, assume the VAR is performed on two series, $\mathbf{r}_t = [i_t, s_t]$, that represent an effected and a shocked series. To be completely clear, the shock is only applied to the shocked variable in the last period and the variable can be rewritten as $\tilde{s}'_t = s_t + \delta_t$. The evolution of both i_t and s_t then proceed as with the earlier reconstruction steps. When $\delta_t = 0$, $\forall t$, there is no change from what was seen before, or $\tilde{i}_{t+n} = i_t + \sum_{j=1}^{n} f_{t+j}$ and $\tilde{s}_{t+n} = s_t + \sum_{j=1}^{n} g_{t+j}$. However, when there is a non-zero shock and the two series have some concurrent linear relationship, the future values of s and i will be affected because $\tilde{s}'_{t+1} = \tilde{s}'_t + \delta_t + g_{t+1}$. To the extent that δ is not just a one period shock, there can be an ongoing decay process that may have a permanent effect. The subsequent evolution of s' and i will have the shock built in recursively depending on the persistence and lags of the series.

---

[113]Semantics are important. The projections shown with the in-sample comparisons do not use data of the actual values. Some researchers might still refer to those as out-of-sample projections but this paper uses the distinction to clarify when no actual values are available to compare with the projections.

Pre-LSAP projections

Both the in-sample and out-of-sample projections rely on a key assumption: projections can accurately estimate actual values. This paper suggests the difference between projected and actual values could represent the magnitude of a monetary treatment, assuming that no other events have an unanticipated effect; however, evidence has not been provided to show that projected values and actual values are close when there is no monetary effect from an LSAP phase.

Figure 9 illustrates the results from several such comparisons when projections are computed in various years and with alternative start dates. The figure relies on the same time series techniques (daily estimations between 10-year Treasury yields and 30-year FRM rates) and specifications (25 day lag structures and 65 day projections) that are used in the paper.

The left panel displays projections that are computed with the same start date (July 17th) but across various years (represented by the different colored lines). The solid lines reflect the actual values while the dotted lines show the projected values. Consider the blue lines that start projections on July 17, 2002. The projected values mimic the actual values at the beginning and some deviation begins after 30 business days (six calendar weeks), but the final projection is only 11 bps above the actual value of 5.84 percent. This panel shows times series of projected and actual values compare between one year versus another and the final values are fairly close even a full quarter later. Still, it is possible that small differences between projected and actual values are due to the start date of July 17th and that concern is addressed in the right panel.

The right panel takes the difference between the final projection and final actual value (the 11 bps mentioned above) and reproduces it across several dimensions. The horizontal axis denotes the year when a start date begins and the vertical axis measures the magnitude of the differences. The plotted values represent differences computed for four start dates: January 17th, July 17th, August 13th, and October 26th.[114] The final 11 bps difference for July 17th is shown in the right panel with a blue triangle in 2002 to correspond with the blue line in the left panel.[115] To be clear, the right panel does not display a time series; the scatter plot illustrates the magnitude of final differences (between predicted and actual values) when different start dates are used across five years before any LSAP phases began. The right panel represents a sample of 20 observations (four start dates and five years) that show projections can come fairly close to actual values regardless of the start date or year. The distribution of all the differences ranges between a 25th-percentile of -18 bps and a 75th-percentile of 20 bps. The mean value is a 2.5 bps difference between the projected and actual value, which supports the idea that a relatively simple VAR model can produce reasonable daily projections as far out as a quarter later.

---

[114]The dates are arbitrary (birthdays of prominent people) and independent of monetary events and announcements. When a start date falls on a weekend, the next business day is used as the start date.

[115]Although other colors do not match, all of the final differences (the gap between solid and dotted lines on day 65) in the left panel are shown with blue triangles in the right panel because they are computed with start dates of July 17th.

Figure 9: Qualifying the projections

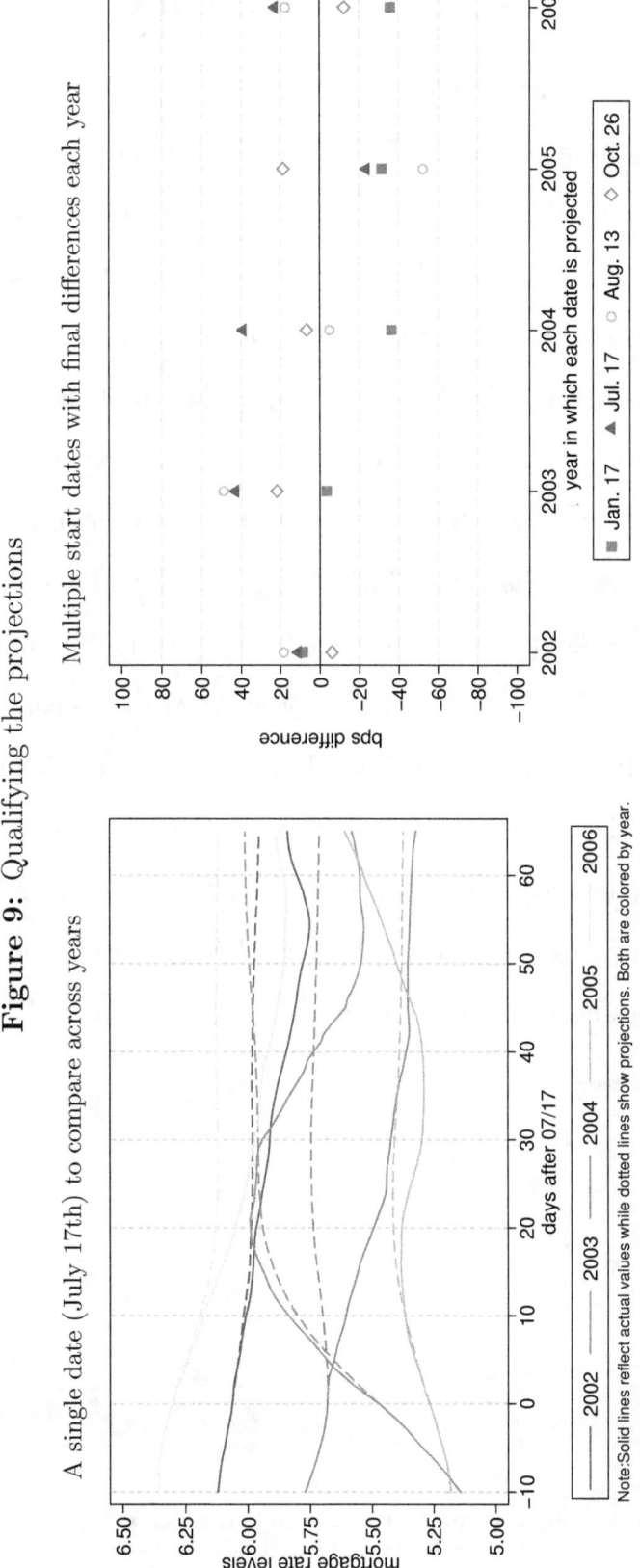

Source: Bloomberg. Projections from authors' calculations. Vertical axes show percentage levels and bps differences.

Appendix D: Shocking additional time series

To provide an example of other market responses, Figure 10 extends the out-of-sample projection approach to several two other financial series. Similar to what is shown in the prior figure, a VAR model of 25 business days is used to calibrate a projection out to 65 business days, or a quarter of a calendar year, with an estimation of interest rates, cumulative LSAP purchases, and the chosen series (in place of the 30-year FRM rate).[116] The differences are projected into levels to show the evolution of the 1-year ARM and the MBS current coupon rate. The same shock scenarios are utilized where the 10-year Treasury Note experiences an unanticipated change of $\pm$ 5, 10, 15, 20, or 25 bps. A shock of +10 bps leads to short-term increase in the 1-year ARM rate and a gain of about 10 bps by the end of the projection (which is 30 bps higher than the final projection value under the no shock scenario). As a short-term debt instrument, the 1-year ARM rate is correlated with its own benchmark ($r = 0.90$), the 1-year Treasury yield, but it even more highly correlated with the 10-year Treasury yield ($r = 0.99$), shows an increase of nearly 100 bps. These additional series demonstrate that unanticipated shocks can be modeled into other financial series but the results are dependent on the quality of the underlying data and the magnitude of the projected long-term shock effect can be substantial.

---

[116]Other lag structures might be more appropriate from a statistical sense but the goal here is to provide a consistent way of obtaining projection estimates. These projections are meant more for informative purposes of describing a general trend rather than exact precision of the point estimates. The fact that in-sample predictions of rates are sometimes within 5 to 10 bps is a testament to the reliability of the approach.

Figure 10: Other out-of-sample projections after shocking 10-year Treasury interest rates

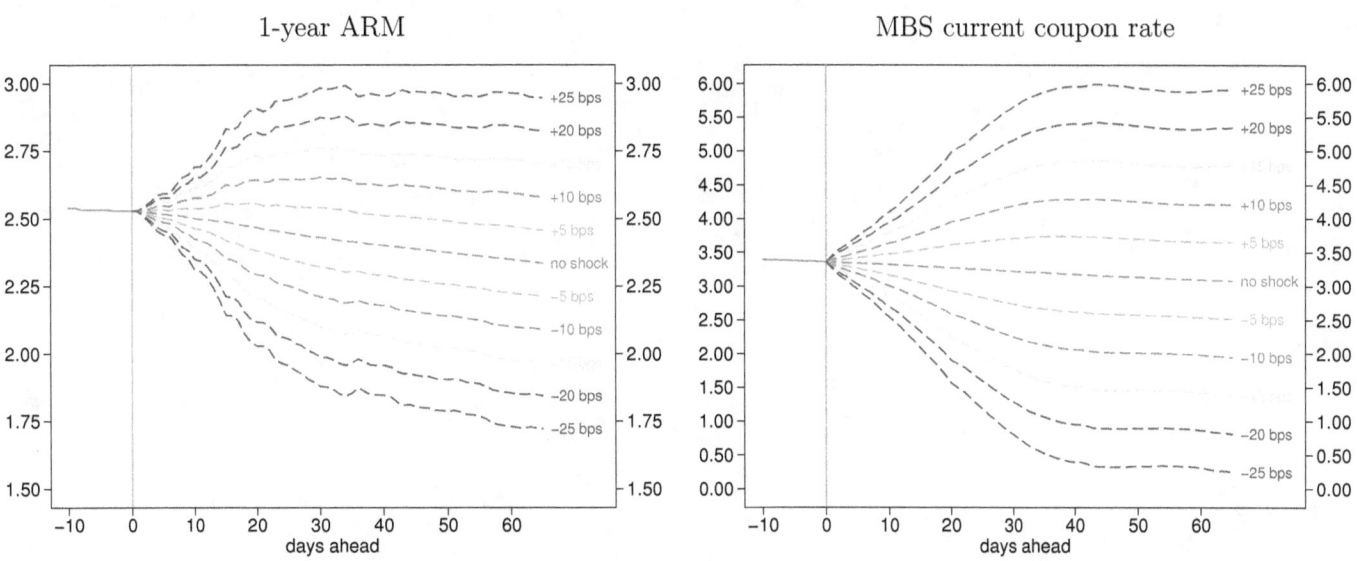

Source: Bloomberg. Projections from authors' calculations. Vertical axes show percentage levels and horizontal axes measure days.